Life After ...
Languages and Literature

T0320971

Thousands of students graduate from university each year. The lucky few have the rest of their lives mapped out in perfect detail – but for most, things are not nearly so simple. Armed with your hard-earned degree the possibilities and career paths lying before you are limitless, and the number of choices you suddenly have to make can seem bewildering.

Life After ... Languages and Literature has been written specifically to help students currently studying, or who have recently graduated, make informed choices about their future lives. It will be a source of invaluable advice and wisdom to graduates (whether you wish to use your degree directly or not), covering such topics as:

- Identifying a career path that interests you – from journalism to interpretation
- Seeking out an opportunity that matches your skills and aspirations
- Staying motivated and pursuing your goals
- Networking and self-promotion
- Making the transition from scholar to worker
- Putting the skills you have developed at university to good use in life

The *Life After ...* series of books are more than simple 'career guides'. They are unique in taking a holistic approach to career advice – recognising the increasing view that, although a successful working life is vitally important, other factors can be just as essential to happiness and fulfilment. They are *the* indispensible handbooks for students considering their future direction in life.

Sally Longson is a life coach and well-known writer and media commentator in the field of careers.

Also available from Sally Longson

Life After ... Art and Design
0-415-37590-8

Life After ... Business and Administrative Studies
0-415-37591-6

Life After ... Engineering and Built Environment
0-415-375920

Life After ... Languages and Literature

A practical guide to life after your degree

Sally Longson

Routledge
Taylor & Francis Group

LONDON AND NEW YORK

First published 2006
by Routledge
2 Park Square, Milton Park, Abingdon, Oxon OX14 4RN

Simultaneously published in the USA and Canada
by Routledge
270 Madison Ave, New York, NY 10016

Routledge is an imprint of the Taylor & Francis Group, an informa business

© 2006 Sally Longson

Typeset in Sabon by
HWA Text and Data Management, Tunbridge Wells
Printed and bound in Great Britain by
TJ International, Padstow, Cornwall

British Library Cataloguing in Publication Data
A catalogue record for this book is available from the British Library

Library of Congress Cataloging-in-Publication Data
Longson, Sally
    Life after – languages and literature: a practical guide to life after
      your degree / Sally Longson.
        p.   cm.
    Includes bibliographical references.
    1. Philology – Vocational guidance.   I. Title
    P60.L66 20006
    402.3′73–dc22   2005036628

ISBN10: 0–415–37593–2
ISBN10: 0–203–08844–1
ISBN13: 978–0–415–37593–1

Contents

Preface

Your degree over – or nearly over – you contemplate your next move, rather like a game of chess. You plot your next move, you fall into it, or someone makes you fall into it. Life is continually like a game of chess, but check-mate – the end result – is entirely where you or someone else decides where it is to be. You can plan to move forward and make progress, or you can feel like a pawn, moved around a board at someone else's bidding.

While you've been studying, the world continues to become a smaller place, thanks to ongoing revolutions in practically every area of life, and most particularly those of information and communications technology and our own attitudes and approach to life. It is more important than ever for all of us to be able to live and work across borders and to speak and empathise with people from other countries. This is good news for you: it should lead to more opportunities to enhance cultural awareness and understanding and teach or train people in foreign languages, or to use your languages to complement your main career. You have that extra something, a skill which can be sold as a service if you are a bit of an entrepreneur, or which can be added as a bonus to an employer's resource.

Governments themselves are increasingly aware of the benefits of having individuals who are skilled in languages. In the UK, the Department for Education and Skills contracted with CILT, the National Centre for Languages, to develop Regional Language Networks to promote languages in the workplace. In Australia, the Government allocated funding to establish a National Centre for Language Training to enable Australia to engage with other countries in business, trade and cultural activities. The European Commission believes that languages have a vital role to play in building a home in which 450 million Europeans can work, live and trade together. It sees the ability to understand and communicate in other languages as a basic skill for all European citizens.

Employers, too, are well aware of the benefits of having a work-force who can talk to customers and clients in their own language. The ethos is changing from *'Well, everyone speaks English'*, to *'we must speak our customers' language'*, an expectation driven by many customers themselves. Many companies are seeing the benefits first hand of having employees who can speak their customers' languages, through increased sales, improved business and personal relationships and a sharper understanding of what the customer wants.

In a world which has become intensively competitive, that tiny bit extra and special care with language can win the day. You have an appreciation of language and literature and the messages it sends out as a result of the tone, words and degree of slang selected, for example. You understand how the use of language can give you clues as to what someone is really thinking and saying, or not saying. You can delve into the rich vocabulary you have to select words which will create a clearer picture or inspire and motivate your colleagues and customers. Your presentations at work will have a special clarity and be easily understood by those who have no knowledge of the subject at hand.

The global economy means that you, the language and literature student, have tremendous opportunities before you if only you can be alert to their potential. Look out across the blue sea and skies before you and cast your mind and eyes to the opportunities beyond them. Life lies before you like a huge ocean. The question is, where are you heading next? Who and what do you want on board?

Having a degree does not guarantee having a good job. *Nothing* in life guarantees you a job. Many graduates expect three years to pass before they secure the permanent professional posts they seek, or move into self-employment. That intervening three years is often spent doing lower level work in administration, retail, leisure and tourism, food and drink, the financial and business services sector, in administration, as sales assistants and pub and bar work. The key to success is to keep your head, and put your career and life goals firmly at the forefront of your mind, focus and efforts. This is all the more important when you consider that there is expected to be a significant increase in the numbers of managers, professional occupations, association professional and technical occupations, and personal service occupations, especially in teaching and research and science, business and public service. Those who persist in their striving for a better career and life will succeed in enjoying one; those who give up will have a lesser quality life than they could have and deserve.

You may land yourself a job – but if you want a *great* job, you need to put in persistent effort to think long term and not to pay day and that you give back as opposed to simply taking. Like any relationships in life, careers need nurturing, and the persistent hard work really only begins when you've started them.

Whatever stage you are at, you're at a great time to assess your life and what you want out of it. Use the exercises in this book to help you determine just that. Careers are only part of life – there are a whole host of other things which are also important, such as relationships, finance and lifestyle. The main emphasis of this book will be on career and work, but you can transfer many of the tips and advice regarding those on to other segments of life. At every turn, opportunities abound for the language and literature graduate, if only you can identify them and position yourself to make them happen. To do this, you'll need to head right out of your comfort zone and take risks to move on and make the most of your life ahead. Let's get started.

Chapter 1

Decisions, decisions ...

What happens now? What happens next?

What happens from now on depends on how determined you are to bring your hopes and aspirations, dreams and ambitions to fruition and the timescale within which you want to do it. Your future plans may be very clear to you, or you may be kicking lots of ideas about, or just not have a clue. What you *do* know is that there are lots of decisions to make and plans to be laid – but what, exactly? Where do you start?

Looking at the next few months

If you've already left university, you may have happily spent the summer enjoying a break at home before considering what happens next. The start of the academic year may feel strange as you realise that for the first time, perhaps in your life, you do not have to go back to school, college or university. You're free to do as you like. This may also be strange to the people you live with, such as your parents. They may not be used to you being around and may start giving you odd jobs to do which interfere with your day and which you may resent. Meal times may be punctuated with discussions about your future and when you're going to get a 'real' job and visitors to the house ask you about your plans. It may feel as though life is going backwards fast, instead of moving on to greater things. Build a structure into your life, even if you have no work or study to go to. Keeping to a routine now will help you when you start work.

You may have studied part time for your degree while holding down a full-time job, working two or three hours a night and trying the patience of family members as you disappear to study yet again. You've probably pleaded with the boss for more time off, spent lunch times doing research on the Internet and sneaked the odd sickie to get that assignment done. And now you're faced with many free hours and you feel a bit lost. It's nice to have a rest from all that study, but having risen to one challenge, you want another.

If you're still at university, *create* time *now* to plan your career. This involves participating in activities such as constructive work experience, internships, develop your web of industry contacts, voluntary work, attending careers and trade events and research into the job market, finding out what resources are available if you want to become self-employed, considering further study, visiting the careers service in person and online, and analysing your own strengths and capabilities. Allocate even three hours a week out of 168 during your degree, and you will be well on the road to securing your immediate future. You'll also have time to fill any missing gaps in your CV to strengthen any future job or course applications and make deadlines. If you are a post-graduate student, this equally applies. Visit your careers service to see how they can help you, and don't leave it too late.

Start building bridges from where you are now to where you want to be. The more foundations you can lay down now, the easier life will be later.

Take control. Get organised

Create a folder – call it something like 'Life After University' – and put everything you need to work on in it. It will save you time searching for pieces of paper and information. If you've got a PC or lap top, create a life and career folder on that, too, for emails and bookmark useful websites you visit regularly. Efficient organisation will clear your mind of clutter and enable you to work more effectively. Your 'life after' folder should grow week by week as you add to it and expand your knowledge, contacts, ideas and work.

Then look ahead

There are several key decisions to make about your life after graduating. These vary from the urgent and/or important, to those things which simply need to be dealt with, such as '*What will I do with all my books and materials?'* and *'Which friends do I want to keep in touch with?'* The latter two questions need to be cleared from your mind, to prevent them from muddying your thinking, so that you can focus on the all-important bigger picture.

There will be urgent decisions you need to make today. The important decisions are not usually time pressured but they affect the Big Picture, i.e. your life. An important and urgent decision may be: do you accept that offer of a post-graduate place you had yesterday? It's Tuesday now, you've got until Thursday at 5 p.m. to decide.

Two major issues which you will almost certainly want to deal with are those of career and finance. Devote more time and energy on these now and you'll reap the rewards in the long term. Socialising may be fun but it won't bring you the best rate of return career-wise, nor will it help you pay off your debts. Building clarity around your future career and life goals will help you strive to towards them. Plotting your career and working up the ladder will bring a higher salary or making progress with your own business will, for example, help you sort out your finances and debts.

Let's follow these two areas in life further.

Do career and financial audits

Table 1.1 demonstrates several questions to ponder.

Doing an audit like this empowers you because you're choosing to address the situation. You're looking at it head on, dealing with known facts rather than assumptions or guesses. You can move forward by creating an action plan and implementing it. With regard to debts, it is better to know what your bottom line is to prevent yourself getting any further into debt. You may have a student debt of £15,000; but how much further are you prepared to allow yourself to build that up before you start paying it back? £20,000? £30,000? It doesn't mean you'll never go for a wild night out with your friends again but it could mean that you look for other ways to have a wild time so that you can control your finances more tightly. Do it jointly with friends in the same boat and work together to deal with it. There are times when we don't like the decisions we have to make, they are uncomfortable and don't fit in well with the lifestyle we want. But discipline never did anyone any harm and can frequently bring unexpected rewards, not least of which are self-respect and an in-built self-belief that you can turn an uncomfortable situation around.

Table 1.1

Career	Finance
What do I want to achieve in life?	How much do I owe?
What is important to me?	Who do I owe it to?
What do have I to offer the world?	How much interest am I paying each
What am I going to do next?	lender monthly?
What could I learn to ensure I get to where I want to be?	What could I do to reduce this interest?
What are my ambitions and aspirations, dreams and hopes?	What incomings do I have now?
	What am I spending it on?
How far do I want a career which uses the knowledge I've acquired of my subject?	What do I have left?
	What could I do to cut back on my spending?
Could I go on to further study?	How could I pay back my loans and
Do I need a break?	debts?
Where in the world do I want to work?	Who could help me?
	What could I do to get the best deal on
How far shall I go in my career?	everything?
Where can I get constructive, informed advice (e.g. university careers service, Prospects)?	What could I do to supplement my income?
	When will I start paying everything back?
Who do I need to support me?	
What action(s) will I take to move me closer to where I want to be?	Where can I get constructive, informed advice (e.g. bank, building society, student loan company)?
	What action(s) will I take to achieve my financial and life goals

Take action now!

1 List the decisions you need to make now and in the next six months.
2 What have you done so far towards making these decisions?
3 What else do you need to do or to know in order to decide? How will you get that information and where will you get it from?
4 Whose help will you need?
5 When do you need to make each decision?
6 What action will you take?

Many of the decisions in one area of our life will impact on others. For instance, your career choice will affect where you live and work, the structure of your life and the people you work with and/or socialise with. It will impact on your standard of living and your overall happiness. You may need to undertake further training, learning and development to acquire your professional status. Career choice can determine the hours you work and whether you're on call or not, the pace of your working day and your stress levels. The effort you put into your career will affect your ability to pay back your loans and start laying strong financial foundations to your life.

Are you an effective decision maker?

You can learn a lot about yourself from the way you've made past decisions. Take two decisions you've made about your university life or course. Ask yourself:

1   What motivated you to take these decisions?
2   *How* did you make them? For example, was it by gut instinct, by careful research and thought, weighing up the pros and cons, tossing a coin, following the lead of others, force of circumstance or meeting the expectations of others? What process did you follow?
3   Who influenced your decisions and subsequent actions? Who could you have involved more or less?
4   What if anything held you back from making decisions and how did you overcome it?
5   Is a pattern emerging about your decision making? What does it tell you about the way you make decisions? Are there patterns which aren't helping you that you need to break?
6   How can you make your decision making more effective?

In making any decision, there are various factors to take into account as shown in Table 1.2.

Decision-making skills transfer well in life, from making career choices to buying a home. Such skills are essential at work, whether you are self-employed, an employee or the boss, in making business decisions such as the clients you choose to work with, which suppliers you choose to work with and whether you should relocate your business to a more cost-effective area. Action plans to implement our decisions are often interrupted by unexpected obstacles which make the journey more of a roller-coaster ride, but a focus on the end result will help steer us through the rougher patches.

Table 1.2

Possible factors influencing your decision	Choosing modules to study	Choosing your career
Your strengths and skills	What you're naturally good at and wanted to build your skills in	Same for career
Your interests	Following your passions	Same for career – this is what you want to do
What was available?	The modules on offer at your university	What is on offer in the region you work in?
Personal fit	You had a lot of time and respect for the tutor and got on well together; you thought he'd bring out the best in you	You like where the company is going and what it stands for; you met the guys and felt comfortable with them
Long-term plans	You want to go into marketing so this fitted well with your career plans	You choose an employer who can meet your aspirations
How you make decisions	for example '…Ran out of time – just ticked the box for something to do' 'Gut feeling. Everything felt right about this'	for example '…Went for the first thing I saw – can always change later' 'The moment I walked into the place, I knew it was right for me'

Focus on the result you want and the obstacles will shrink

Often when faced with a decision, we tend to focus too much on possible problems and the negative. *'There are too many graduates…'*, *'not enough time in the day…'*, *'I don't want to…'* Problems have a way of shrinking when put into the context of what we really want. Let's say you get the offer of a dream career from an employer you'd love to work for. The only hitch is that you don't know anyone in the town you'd be living in. It's a totally new area to you. *'Where will I live if I go somewhere new?'* you may ask. But compared to the job offer, which you're wild with excitement about, the accommodation problem is minor. You know you'll sort it somehow. You could lodge for a while as you look. Your new colleagues may know about housing opportunities and good inexpensive places to live. There will be local papers, the HR department may be able to help you or your new boss. You may have friends in the area from university. The most important thing is that you've got the offer you wanted. You found somewhere to live at university; you can do it again.

Have faith in your own ability to create a life for yourself even if you move to a place where you don't know anyone

Yes, it's hard, but you've done it before and survived. You've handled these problems before and you can do so again, thanks to those transferable skills you developed at university, such as the abilities to:

1 start completely afresh – new people, new place, new things to learn, new challenges;
2 take part in and contribute to an organisation – previously, your university, now the workplace, the community, new friends;
3 find your way around and learn the ropes;
4 ask the right questions of the right people to get the answers you need;
5 network and get to know people across the organisation – as you did at university;
6 take the initiative and making things happen – a day at university or college which – lectures and tutorials apart – was pretty much your own;
7 show how adaptable and flexible you are in juggling work, study and social activities, often changing plans at the last minute;
8 organise your time;
9 hunt out new friends and like-minded people you can particularly relate to;
10 relate to people of all different sorts of backgrounds, nationalities and abilities.

University has taught you to think, to question, to be creative, to think laterally, to challenge, to research, to find solutions to problems and to interact. Those skills will never be wasted. And the more you stretch yourself and expand them, the more powerful a resource they will become.

Wait a minute ...

Before you start making decisions, consider what's really important to you.

Where are you going? How does the decision fit into the bigger picture?

A key starting point to making successful decisions involves knowing what is right for you in life or work. You need a strong sense of self-worth and self-awareness. These things encompass areas such as the roles you want to play in life, your career interests, ambitions, aspirations, the environments and conditions you thrive in and learn best in, the things you need around you to make you happy and feel fulfilled and those things that are important to you and what you couldn't do without, i.e. your values. Know what you want, and life has more purpose. You'll move faster because you don't deviate from your route spending time doing things you don't want to do. Many people simply wait for that lucky break to knock on their door. Unfortunately, they have a long wait. You can create your own luck, as Dr Wiseman points out in his excellent book *The Luck Factor* (see Further Reading at the end of this book).

What's important to you?

When you live by your values, you look forward to the start of a new day or week, and you wake up with a happy heart. Life feels right, you feel fulfilled with a strong sense of your own self-worth. Your goals, hopes and aspirations seem easier to strive for because you're at your best as you work towards them. You know you're making the right choices and decisions and moving in the right direction. Similarly, the company which recruits staff with values equal to its own has a good feel about it. The staff are happy, motivated, fulfilled and feel appreciated. They look forward to going to work and are a tight-knit team.

Five signs when life – and work in particular – does not encapsulate your values are:

1   You can't perform properly. You get very tired trying to work at something that doesn't gel with you while pretending that all is well.
2   You're frustrated and short tempered, especially as a new working week looms.

3   It's lonely. Everyone else seems to be on a different wave length to you.

4   You keep thinking, *There must be more to life than this!* This thought persists over time, making you increasingly frustrated and more angry.

5   You're disappointed in yourself because you know that you should cut your losses and leave, but you can't take find the *courage* to do it.

Of course, you may find the perfect match and then something hinders its progression: a technological innovation, a change in the markets, a drop in demand, restructuring, redundancy. Employers understand that it takes time to find the right match, and when reading your CV, they consider your achievements, progression, development, future career plans and the person who lies behind the words on paper and portfolio. But it's your responsibility to find the right career and role.

Table 1.3 gives examples of life and career values. Which ones are important to you to have or be in your life and career to make you truly happy and feel successful?

Having considered which values are important to you, you can build a life and career which incorporates them. For example, if

Table 1.3

Winner	Participant	Contributor
Continuous change	Change where needed	Little change
Security	Stability	Risk
Creativity	Performer	Conformity
Compassion	Fair	Faith
Achiever	Influencer	Supporter
Recognition	Status in community	Appreciated
Success	Work–life balance	Fulfilment
Autonomy	Independence	Managed
Visionary	Implement	Support
Adventure	Spirituality	Pleasure
Driver, creator	Follow the leader	Win–win
Wealth	Rewarded	Feel-good factor
Happiness	Freedom	Other

achievement is very important to you, you could look for careers where results are exceedingly important and measured, such as sales roles.

Select the top eight values which are essential to you from those you've ticked above and create a picture of what they mean to you – don't make any assumptions about them. Get the foundations right. If you think that things such as travel, holidays and a good social life are your values, consider what those things *give you* or *provide you with* and you'll have your real values. Then rank those eight in order. Which one is most important? Which values could you *not* do without? And which are you *not* prepared to compromise on?

Compromising in life will bring more win–wins

At some stage in life, you'll need to compromise. For example, let's say you want to work for an ethical company, but the only position you were offered in six months was from a company which was, in your eyes, unethical, what would you do? Would you refuse to take the job and uphold your values or take the offer up and move on as soon as you could?

What happens now?

Figure 1.1 poses questions to ask yourself.

Many graduates have no clear idea of what they want to do after university, so they take whatever comes their way in the first three to five years after graduation, as shown in Figure 1.2.

This runway to career take-off may be longer and tougher in terms of getting that lucky break, the opportunity or gap in the market, especially as you are probably trying to begin a new life at the same time. You may hook a lower-level job, just to get going, and you'll need a real rocket thrust of persistent effort to get yourself to where you aspire to be. Keep focused on your goal, and you'll head in the right direction. If you lose that focus, your ambitions will take longer to achieve, or they may lose their impetus and fizzle out.

Do you want a job, a career or a business?

These are very different things. Jobs fit well into short-term plans and bring the money in, but they don't necessarily stretch you or pay well. Consequently they can make you feel bored and disillusioned, especially when you weigh up your salary against your stu-

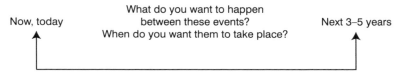

- Within five years, working abroad for a global company
- More of a strategic role with the company I'm with now
- Have professional qualifications in a business function supported by my languages
- Use my knowledge and language skills to help small companies expand overseas
- Get qualified as a translator with a view to setting up my own business
- Working in China as a website localiser
- Qualified as a ...
- Paid off ...% of my student loans and started to ...
- Settled down into life after university
- Found my partner for life

Figure 1.1

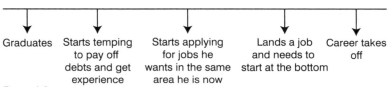

Figure 1.2

dent debts. Careers run over a course of time, enabling you to develop your skills, expertise and experience in one particular sector, often climbing the career ladder to reach the upper echelons of the business and sector. You may have a view of the top of this ladder from the bottom or you may create the view, rung by rung, as you climb up. Of course, a job can become a career if you take the initiative, yank it up a gear and get yourself noticed, i.e. take two rungs at once. You could also decide to set up your own business, which enables *you* to make all the decisions: what you will sell, the who, what, when, why, how and where.

By the end of your life, you may have had all of these.

How does your career fit into your life?

You need to find the work–life balance that's right for you, your life and your dependants. At first, this may be hindered as you devote time to establishing yourself and getting a foot on the work and housing ladders, putting bricks and blocks down to get the life you want – the house, family life, network of friends, security, professional qualifications where appropriate, the opportunity for advancement and professional growth, recognition and appreciation. You may prefer to focus on having fun, rather than sorting out your career and life. *Well, there's always next year.*

A hunger for success at work can seriously impact on our quality of life. If your goal was to make your first million within three years after leaving university, and you succeeded, but you lost all your friends in the process because you were always working, would you still deem that a success? Some graduate programmes demand that you dedicate 60, 70, 80 or even 90 per cent of your life to work. You may be prepared to give that early in your career if it takes you to where you really want to be, or you may prefer to opt for a more sensible work–life balance which takes you to a rung on the ladder which you're happy with.

What matters is the *degree of control* we each have over our work–life balance. If you decide to work 100 hours a week to make that first million, that's your choice. Work–life balance becomes an issue when we feel we *don't* have a choice; that other people are making decisions for us about the hours we need to put in. Some employers place a higher priority on work–life balance than others. The most demanding employer may be the person who runs their own business.

As you create a vision of your future career, build specifics into the picture so that you can build plans around them. For example:

- What is your career goal, outcome or end result? If it makes things easier, look at this over a three- to five-year period.
- Why is this important to you?
- How exactly is your career important to you?
- Where do you want to be doing it?
- When are your timescales/deadlines for achieving your goal?
- Who will you be doing it with?
- Who can help you?
- How will you get there? What are the different ways you could reach the outcome you want?
- What can you do to boost your chances of success?
- What can you control? What is outside your control?
- Which deadlines do you need to look out for, such as applying for post-graduate courses, work experience placements and internships?

- What in life and in your career are you *not* prepared to risk, e.g. your integrity, values, standards, expectations of yourself, key relationships ... and what *are* you prepared to risk.

The *why* is important. If you don't understand *why* something is important to you, it is far less likely to happen. If you understand how a goal relates to your values – for example, keeping fit is important to you because you value good health which gives you the freedom to live your life to the full – then you're more likely to achieve it.

Wherever you are, pinpoint careers help available to you

Find out what careers advisory services are available to you where you are *now*, face-to-face, online and by telephone. Sometimes you just need to sit down and talk through your future with someone whom you can trust and who is impartial, qualified and trained. Tap into local universities and colleges, your old university and other private agencies in your area for access to careers information and support. Most higher education institutions allow graduates to use their facilities for up to two or three years after graduation and they may also help graduates from any university wishing to move into, remain in or return to their area. You may be charged for some services.

Finally, don't forget that your degree has taught you many transferable skills. Use the forward and strategic planning skills you acquired throughout your degree experience to plan your career and life. Take the initiative and put your brain and energy to work.

Summary action points

Look back at your life overall:

1   How much has it consisted of what you want so far? What efforts have you put in to make sure that happened?
2   What lessons have your past choices taught you as you look to your future?
3   What do you want to achieve *in your life* in the next five years? What would that mean to you?

Chapter 2

Creating your career

This chapter is all about helping you to create a vision of what you want your career to consist of. Even if you already have a picture, use the self-assessment exercises to add depth to it. Stand back and look at yourself, as if you were looking at the ground from a helicopter, and the distance will help you think more clearly.

Careers using languages can have a high degree of flexibility and opportunity, if looked at in a positive light, and you can carve and create your own career path. If you crave more structure and security, then take that into account when looking at the various choices ahead of you. As a graduate of modern languages and literature, you have a huge range of possibilities ahead of you, so rather than trundle through them one by one, it may be more helpful to pose some searching questions to yourself as a way of finding where your future lies.

Things to consider when choosing your career

Focus on your:

- passions and motivators;
- ambitions;
- preferred role at work;
- desired results;
- preferred skills;
- interests;
- desire to work with particular people or group;
- preferred products;
- desire to use your degree subject;
- chosen lifestyle;

♦ what really counts in a career for you.

What are your passions and motivators?

If you want to be happy and successful in your career, get passionate. Find something to do which really inspires and motivates you and stirs you to action, which gives you a real buzz. This is all about your vocation and reason for working.

- ♦ What excites you and inspires you?
- ♦ What are you passionate about?
- ♦ What do you want to make a difference to or particularly do something about?
- ♦ How do you want to make a difference to the world, a local community or a group of people?
- ♦ What secret dreams and aspirations do you have?
- ♦ What makes you jump out of bed in the morning?

How far do you want to climb up the career ladder?

Take a long-term view of your career. The following are all examples of a successful career. When you look back on yours, do you want any of them to feature?

- ♦ I was a partner in a professional firm
  Accountancy, lawyer
- ♦ I ran my own business
  Trainer specialising in the recruitment sector,
  ran a language school
  advised small companies on exporting to Asia
- ♦ We were the number one provider of ...
  Soft toys, computer equipment, language books
- ♦ I've helped a lot of individuals on a one-to-one basis
  I train businessmen in Russian
- ♦ I got to the top of my profession
  I was well known as an expert in sign language/customs of the
  area
- ♦ I got the work–life balance I wanted and time for those things which were important to me
  Public sector – I was a manager in the health service

- I've given back a great deal
  Volunteering in local Citizens Advice Bureau helping with languages
- I didn't have a traditional career. I went against the grain a lot, buck the trend, did it my way
  Volunteer working overseas
- I was a trouble-shooter. People came to me to turn situations around
  Interim manager, management consultant
- I made a difference.
  Teacher
- Other ...

What role do you want to have?

Look at this question now, then fast forward in your mind to three to five years' time. Which role(s) do you see yourself playing? People play different roles at work: if you are self-employed, you may be the company owner, managing the books and marketing *and* doing the work to achieve the results you want. Each of the roles below contribute to an organisation but in different ways. Which of the roles outlined in Table 2.1 appeal to you?

Weigh up the pros and cons of each role. Which ones reflect your key values? They all call for different qualities and values.

Other questions to ask is what level you want to work at.

1   In the professional, senior manager and associate professional bracket?
2   At the administrative and secretarial level?
3   Starting in the administration and secretarial level intending to move up? (This move will demand huge focus and effort. Note that some administrative roles in the public and education sector are graduate positions from the outset.)
4   For yourself, where you may be creating the vision for your business, making it happen and doing the administration.

The pros of moving up the career ladder include better pay and perks, being able to contribute to the company's direction, and helping your team grow and progress. There are cons, too including management responsibilities which may take you away from the work you really want to do, and they will almost certainly follow

Table 2.1

Leader	*Technician*
the boss	doing the technical aspects as op-
team leader	posed to strategic and business
	planning
Team player	*Back office*
working with a group of people to	administration, ensuring things run
achieve a particular goal or mission	smoothly, e.g. office support, office
	manager, PA, operations
Employee	*Entrepreneur*
bank, building society	creating a business out of a vision
Manager	*Freelance support*
project manager	providing a service or product to
implementing vision	businesses as and when required
Company owner	*Front line*
e.g. small business owner	client-relationship managers
	bankers

you home. Once you are fully effective at one level, you can look to climb to the next rung, either taking a long-term view and heading up from the outset or making your way up step by step. As you progress, leadership and management skills, the ability to communicate and empathise become even more important. Strategic thinking, forward planning, being decisive and risk taking will feature highly as you rise to the top of a company.

Look to back office roles, as well!

Some back office roles may not be the sexy front-line roles that many graduates crave, yet businesses cannot function without them, and changes in technology and the structure of organisations have made them far more interesting. They offer scope to those who can influence and negotiate with others, who can argue their point and can take the initiative and spot what needs to be done and do it. We're talking collecting data, analysing it and making recommendations, often across departments; and project managers who can implement programmes, with strong IT, time management and people skills. Roles such as company secretary, compliance, human resources, IT, office manager, and finance all have much to offer.

There's more to these roles than meets the eye

An example is an Executive Assistant or Personal Assistant, supporting and working closely with senior management. Some people in these posts have great influence, determining who should have access to their boss and when, delegating much of his or her work to other senior managers, liaising with the Board including captains of industry, and having control of budgets, sometimes in their millions. Many entrepreneurs want sharp, commercially oriented graduate calibre and frequently bi-lingual PAs or EAs, capable of delegating, organising, managing, networking, researching, analysing and presenting arguments and writing presentations. The PA role can be a great place to launch your career from and gain insight into organisations and sectors, but you need to focus on your long-term goals to ensure that you keep progressing towards them. A downside of the role is that you may be working alongside other PAs who are not graduates. Many employers are, however, looking for new routes to recruit PAs or EAs with a high degree of intellect, initiative, leadership and excellent communication skills.

Does your idea of career success incorporate professional qualifications?

If your answer is yes, it does, be prepared to devote extra hours after a long day's work to study and train, attend courses, sit examinations, undertake projects and do research. You'll commit two or three nights a week study, plus most weekends. With good time management, discipline and focus, you can do it, just as many students have done before you. Once achieved, professional qualifications cannot be taken away from you. And they open doors. Many companies have professionally qualified people on their Boards. But, as in any game, you need a strategy to get there.

What do you want to achieve and consequently contribute to an organisation's mission?

What sort of results and achievements really turn you on and give you that feel-good factor and buzz? What would you need to be doing to achieve them? How would you measure your success in terms of the contribution you make to your employer and his/her clients? What do you want to contribute to the world, the sector, your employer, the team and customers or clients? Examples of results are shown in Table 2.2.

As you work through the exercises in this chapter, look to see how they all add up together. For example:

Take a result which is important to you   e.g. meeting targets
Add it to a sector which interests you   e.g. property
                                         e.g. equestrian world
Preferred role: e.g. leader
                                         e.g. front line with
                                             customer
Possible results: e.g. estate agency
                                         e.g. blood stock sales

How hungry are you to make these results happen?

Look at the results you've highlighted. Are you ravenous to take them on board, or just wanting to nibble at them? How fulfilled

Table 2.2

Clinching the deal/sale Recruitment/sales	*Exceeding targets* Sales, estate agents
Influencing groups Public policy, decision maker	*Influencing individuals* Teaching, social work, youth work, policy writers, back office
Strong motivated team Manager, coach, team building events	*New policy/procedure* Manager
Idea going into fruition Creator, innovator	*Recognition (from whom?)* Politician
Influencing the direction of something Strategist, entrepreneur	*Justice* Law, welfare officer
A new look Designer, creator, public relations	*Happy customers* Customer care agent
Recommendations followed through Researcher	*Huge profits* Financial officer
Takeover of a company Investment banker	*Making a difference to a country/the world*
Developing others Manager, coach, trainer, team leader	*Other*

would you be if you were hungry and driven enough to achieve the results you wanted every working day, 48 weeks of the year? You need that hunger and passion to make an impact and get the results you want. If you nibble at something, it will be less fulfilling, so look for a cause, a passion, interest or aspiration which really hits the spot.

What does the picture of success look like to you?

Do you see a healthy bank account, flashy car, exotic holidays and so on? Or is it more about leaving the office having done something great for the good of society or a charity that day; the feel-good factor is more important than pay and a wealthy lifestyle.

What do you want to do and what skills do you want to use to make these results happen?

Skills your degree gave you include: working on your own or with a group; the abilities to read, write, listen and speak in a language different to your own, with an understanding of the grammatical rules and vocabulary; and to translate and interpret. You'll be comfortable using these skills in various formal and informal settings through various medium under pressure such as email, writing letters and reports, talking on the telephone and through conferencing facilities. You can use primary and secondary sources, such as dictionaries, library and bibliographic terms and the Internet, and the skill to interpret them with local nuances. You have a powerful and sensitive understanding of your own language and how it can be used to maximum effect, whilst you also enjoy the ability to listen carefully to the words someone uses in their speech or writing. In short, you can de-code language.

Graduates of languages and literature degrees excel at developing their own linguistic skills through the most effective route for them to learn. You can empathise with different cultures and people, and you understand how different countries approach business, economics, society, law, science or politics, or how they have come into being through their historical and geographical and literary past. Your studies will have given you considerable knowledge of and familiarity with a country's customs, and how they compare with those of your own. This boosts your tolerance of others, and your ability to relate to people, an asset in any management and leadership role.

You're disciplined and you can concentrate over long periods of time, with an excellent memory and close attention to detail. The study of grammar will have given you a logical and systematic approach to work and projects. If you've lived abroad you'll be very self-reliant and used to moving to other places and quickly settling in, invaluable if you've got to re-locate on the job.

Many skills are transferable, such as communicating, i.e. you can transfer them from one job to another. Equally, most jobs demand specific job-related skills. A language trainer, for example, will focus on skills such as: business development and possibly cold calling; negotiating her charges; assessing the needs of employer and employees receiving the training; planning and delivering it; monitoring and reviewing her clients' progress; and evaluating further training needs.

Table 2.3 gives examples of both transferable and job specific skills.

Using the skills in Table 2.3 as a guide, consider the following questions.

1 Which skills have you developed or practised through your university life and academic studies? Build a picture around them.
2 Which skills would apply to any graduate of any discipline (i.e. are transferable)?
3 Look back to three achievements you are proudest of. Which skills did you use to make them happen?
4 Which skills do you want to use in the future?
5 Which careers need those skills? For example, if you would like to communicate over the telephone regularly, a career in headhunting or sales may suit, as you need to do a lot of cold calling.

The last question is the most difficult because you need a basic overview of the careers market to start identifying your slot. A programme such as Prospects Planner (www.prospects.ac.uk) may help you make the link between your skills and possible good career matches.

Table 2.3

Achieving	Evaluating	Presenting
Acquiring	Finding solutions	Pricing
Administering	Fundraising	Problem solving
Advising	Guiding	Processing
Analysing	Helping	Producing
Answering	Identifying	Programming
Applying	Implementing	Project management
Assembling	Influencing	Promoting
Assessing	Innovating	Qualitative skills
Building	Inspiring	Quantitative skills
Buying	Interviewing	Questioning
Caring	Inventing	Recommending
Challenging	Investigating	Researching
Classifying	Keeping records	Securing
Coaching	Learning	Selecting
Cold calling	Liaising	Selling
Communicating	Listening	Servicing
Conducting discussions	Locating	Setting targets
Conserving	Making	Studying
Consulting	Managing	Summarising
Counselling	Marketing	Supervising
Creating	Mentoring	Supporting
Critical thinking	Monitoring	Taking risks
Dealing	Motivating	Talking
Debating	Negotiating	Teaching
Designing	Networking	Teamworking
Detecting, e.g. false	Numeracy	Training
logic	Operating	Understanding
Developing	Organising	Watching
Diagnosing	Persuading	Winning
Displaying	Planning	Writing
Distributing	Preparing	Other

What sector do you want to work in and what knowledge do you want to work with?

If you've got language and linguistic skills, you could work in any sector, but choose one which interests you. The choices you made during your degree could provide you with hints as to the sector you would like to work in. You may have acquired a very high level of knowledge already in a particular subject or studied a range of options which gave you an overall expertise. These choices can point you in the direction of future careers. For example:

Knowledge	Potential sectors
Politics +	Local government, international organisations, research institutes
Current affairs	Journalism, politics, national government, EU, NATO
Business	Corporates, small businesses, web globaliser, recruitment agencies
Literature +	Teaching
Language	Media, journalism, web localiser, IT

Think about what interests you and turns you on. In any sector, there will be a huge range of niche and specialist areas which will require your skills so research it thoroughly to find the right role for you. Let's take the world of education as an example. The tendency is automatically to think of teaching in primary and secondary school. But you may not like small children (which rules out primary education) and you may be anxious about the thought of being faced with 30 spotty adolescents with raging hormones (such as you would meet in secondary schools). The reality is that teaching has far more opportunities than primary and secondary education, as shown in Figure 2.1.

In each case, you will deal with different people, perhaps one or several of the following:

1   Business/organisation to business/organisation such as providing cultural advisory services.
2   Business to customer, in which case you're selling your company's goods to a customer – such as teaching a creative writing course to adults on holiday;
3   Customer to customer, for example, training a businessman in basic Chinese.
4   Public sector or voluntary organisations, or international bodies and governments, such as prisoners who may need to learn basic reading and writing.

You can develop a truly specific career and base yourself in the retail sector, leisure, tourism, travel, or whatever, but you can choose the customers and clients you want to provide a service or product to.

Imagine your preferred client group – for example, let's assume you're a language trainer. Who would you engage with in the course

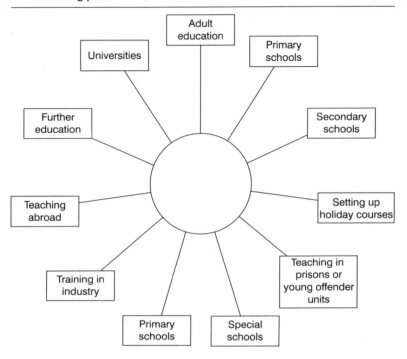

Figure 2.1

of your business? Language trainers may teach adults; but they may also deal with language schools, employers, exam boards, fellow tutors and the like as part of the day-to-day routine of making the job happen. Most choose to specialise in a particular niche, such as law, finance, employment, etc. This puts them in direct contact with a particular sort of client or customer. The trainer will need to keep up-to-date with everything that is happening in that sector and have a strong network within it.

What sort of clients and customers do you want to work for?

This can affect the ethos and being of the organisation, be it private, public or voluntary sector. It can affect your pay, long-term working conditions and the sort of work you do. Some offer the promise of a better work–life balance; public and voluntary organisations tend to be better at this than the private sector. Examples of potential employers could be:

- community
- government
- private sector
- charity
- international organisation
- yourself
- social enterprise
- dot.com
- micro-business (under 5)
- small businesses (5–49)
- medium-sized business (50–250)
- large business (250–499)
- corporate (500+)

There will be institutions and research organisations, national, European, Asian, American, Australasian or global, who need graduates with an in-depth, working knowledge of another country and its language and culture. There will also be the small business, the entrepreneur who sees a business opportunity and wants to go for it but needs someone with the language expertise.

The front-line client-focused role will have far greater liaison with external clients. Some companies focus on specific industries (e.g. most of their clients are in the food and drink sector). An interest in those sectors will help you keep up-to-date and impress your client with your knowledge. Many recruitment agencies specialise in a specific sector, such as education, media, finance and charities. So consider who you want your clients and customers to be and the products you want to work with. Don't forget that smaller companies need specialist services too. Theatres, studios, community programmes, festivals, educational specialists, galleries, orchestras, publishers, bookstores, councils and museums will all need marketing, finance, HR, organisers and planners, so even if you develop these specialist niches elsewhere first, you can always transfer to work for them later, perhaps by going freelance.

Are there specific products or areas of expertise you want to work with?

Managing involves taking control of something, being in charge of it. The workplace is full of managers (some would say too many), and there are opportunities for the specialist (finance, human resources, facilities), or more of a generalist incorporating several of these. Table 2.4 gives examples of the areas of work you might manage.

Table 2.4

Money, budgets	*Laws/regulations*
General management	Health and safety
Finance	Compliance
Accountancy	Company secretary
Banks, building societies	Human Resources
Financial advisers	
People	*Ideas*
Training and Development	Product development
Human Resources	Design and creativity
Recruitment	Advertising
Teaching	Business development
Lecturing	Innovation
Training/coaching	Enterprise
Targets	*Products, technical expertise*
Recruitment	Marketing
Sales	Research and development
Customer service	Distributing
	Buyer
Processes	*Systems*
Product development	IT
Disaster management	Disaster management
Distribution manager	
Events/Conferences/Exhibitions	*Words/language*
Selling	Journalism
Organising	Publishing
Advertising	Technical author
Services	*Buildings*
Marketing	Facilities management
Customer service	Health and safety
Insurance	Operations management
Building surveyor	

Of course you can take this further, dividing it into niches. Thus you could work for a recruitment company specialising in multi-lingual staff in sales, or one which focused on education. It all depends on what position excites you in the marketplace.

How relevant do you want your career to be to your degree?

The questions thus far in this chapter have asked you to pinpoint things which are important to you in terms of your ambition, aspiration, knowledge and people you want to work with and for.

Let's consider how far you want to apply the knowledge and skills you learnt on your degree course to the workplace. This decision can profoundly affect your career choice and the opportunities before you. Which applies to you?

I want to:

- Use all my degree knowledge and apply it every day to the work I'm doing?
- Take an aspect of my degree studies and focus on that.
- Use my language skills to enable me to do my job more effectively – my languages are part of my tool-kit.
- Keep my languages as a hobby and interest – they'll be handy for watching films and socialising.
- Have a career which encompasses fully my skills with the written and spoken word.

Take up a career directly related to your degree

Many careers enable you to use your language skills but they will differ, depending on how much contact you want with people. If you work with people one-to-one, or as a group, as a teacher or trainer, you'll have more contact time with people than you would if you were, for example, translating films. A publisher spots opportunities in the market, identifies those books which will sell, works with authors and those involved in the process of putting a book together. An editor would do far more writing and editing.

There are a number of careers relating directly to languages where language and literature really are placed squarely at the centre of your daily work. Here are some examples of them.

Translating – working with the written word

Since the number of ways with which we communicate has expanded (to include email, the Internet, websites, advertorials, video conferences) so has the number of niche areas in which a translator might work. You could specialise in any number of areas, such as documents, books, films with subtitles, voice-overs and dubbing.

You could undertake simultaneous translating, perhaps for a conference where delegates speak in their own language and the interpreter immediately translates, or conservative translating, where a speaker makes breaks in the presentation for you, the interpreter, to relay the information.

Interpreter – working with people and the spoken word

As more of us work with others of all different nationalities and organisations and increasingly work across borders, so the opportunities for translators and interpreters should rise. You could provide interpreting services for:

- visitor support for those new to an area, for example people who have been relocated by their companies;
- large international corporations who employ interpreters and translators;
- conferences and big events where you are simultaneously translating or interpreting while the main speakers are talking;
- hotels;
- tourist guides.

Becoming a cultural adviser

This a growing area, where businesses give travellers advice on the customers and culture of a country and help them prepare for a successful (business) trip, perhaps accompanying them to act as interpreters and translators.

Working with the public sector

If you have local community languages or the British Sign Language or the more commonly used languages, the police, courts, public health and local government could enlist your services. The National Register of Public Service in the UK (http://www.nrpsi.co.uk) enables linguists to provide details of their services to the public sector, provided that they have fulfilled various criteria. You may be called out in the early hours of the morning to provide a service for a local emergency service.

Training

Training offers multiple opportunities, since many companies sending employees on business at least prefer them to be able to make introductions and small talk in the language of their client, even if the latter speaks excellent English. As you know, it helps to have confidence if you can get the gist of what a document is referring to, even if you need to get a final confirmation from an expert translator.

Training consultant

Many companies recognise that they need to train their staff in languages, but simply have no idea where to start. Training consultants advise companies as to the best ways to train their staff in the use of languages. In this case, you may not be using your language skills as much as your business acumen and training awareness.

Going local

A relatively new profession is that of web design localisers, whereby web designers help businesses make their brand, products and services easily understood in countries where they want to sell products.

Working with words

Figure 2.2 shows just how specialist a field can be.

Again, there are key questions you need to weigh up:

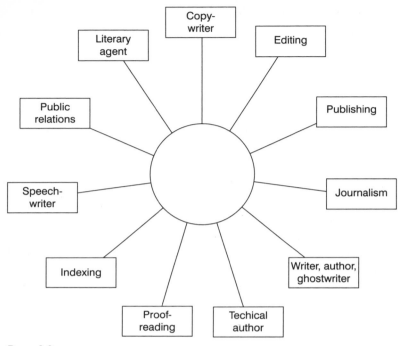

Figure 2.2

- ◆ What subject matter do you want to cover? Generalist, such as a community newspaper, or specialist, such as sports, finance, travel?
- ◆ What sort of medium do you want to work on, e.g. magazines, newspapers, online providers of news and features, radio, television?
- ◆ How do you want to set yourself up, e.g. as a freelance or working for someone else?

To get into the field of your choice, be prepared to be a generalist at first, moving to specialise later on.

Aside from your language skills, you'll need core competences and soft skills

Whether you set up on your own or work for someone else, you will still need to demonstrate your skills in areas such as:

1   Time management: identifying your priorities, meeting dead-lines, giving time to what is important (such as business development activities).

2   Business development: pitching for and winning business; negotiating skills; building client relationships; obtaining feedback on your services and how they can be improved and enhanced; networking; creating a vision and deciding how to implement it.

3   Commercial awareness: an understanding of how business works (and an ability to speak the corporate language).

4   Self-promotion skills and the ability to inspire confidence (people often feel nervous when learning a language for example).

5   Communication skills, cultural awareness, tact, diplomacy and firmness.

6   The ability to drive forward your own continued career development: technical expertise, business know-how, IT knowledge where appropriate, changes and trends in the workplace.

7   For the self-employed: administration, book-keeping, budgeting, business development, sales, marketing, advertising and PR skills, plus networking and negotiating.

Use your language skills to complement your main role

Language and literature students go into a wide variety of careers. The questions posed in the first part of this chapter will help you identify the career you want, because languages and literature will transfer over to any of them. There are institutions and research organisations who need graduates with an in-depth, working knowledge of another country and its language and culture. This means you could go into areas such as sales, marketing, accountancy, consultancy, IT, financial services, media, travel, tourism, voluntary work and management, all of which could have their own specific niche. You may have a professional qualification in your area of expertise but your language abilities will boost your effectiveness on the job. Languages really come alive when you combine using them with your expertise in another field.

Example

German-born Johannes works for a finance company and he is based in its office in Milan. In a typical week, he speaks Italian, French, English and his own language in business meetings and social settings. In five working days one week, he worked in four major cities, took six flights, two of which were long haul, and he annoyed his partner again through having to cancel social engagements because of work. Johannes' role involves so much unexpected travel that he always carries a change of essential clothing, plus passport, cash and credit card. But his language skills are not his main area of expertise. They simply complement his banking and interpersonal skills, and enable him to do his job highly effectively.

If, like Johannes, you want an international position in a global company, you need to be able to function effectively in a multicultural environment. You'll need to be adaptable, flexible, sensitive, tenacious, a risk taker and have lots of initiative. You'll need to be prepared to work outside of your comfort zone and have a great sense of humour and patience – working abroad can have lots of hit-and-miss days owing to hitches in air travel, 4 a.m. conference calls and dealing with different cultures. You'll need to be prepared to work abroad, often at short notice; your family and friends will need to be pretty stoical too. You need to be able to work across borders and create good working relationships fast and to have a strong interest in world affairs. Some companies will send you abroad sooner than others – a large corporate could send you for training in the USA, for example, whereas a small company might send you on your first business trip to Belgium in the first few weeks.

Get a feel for how global a company is – where are its clients coming from, for example, and does it have any partnership companies elsewhere or does it see itself expanding overseas in the years ahead? How might that impact on the career and life opportunities available to you?

How do you see your career and lifestyle fitting in together?

Consider how you see your career and lifestyle intertwining. For example, a language trainer may need to give a session at 7 a.m. one morning in a location which demands him leaving home at 5.30 a.m. This could have an impact on any plans the previous evening.

Travelling with a job may sound very exciting, and it can give you great experience and new friends, but it can also be quite lonely. Do any of the following appeal?

- Travelling all the time, e.g. sales consultant continually on the road
  Sales consultant, senior manager
- Working in another country with an occasional visit home
  Anything you want to be!
- Needing expert knowledge about the culture of another country
  Ambassador, adviser, reporter, journalist
- Working with people of different cultures and customs
  Travel industry, UN, EU
- Using your language skills as a central role in the job
  Translator, interpreter
- Working for a company which will give you the opportunity to work abroad
  Accountancy in a large global company
- Working abroad for a couple of years in one office
  Large global company
- Working for a political international organisation
  NATO, UN, EU, diplomat, MEP
- Helping under-developed countries, often working in very difficult and dangerous conditions
  VSO, disaster management
- Improving international relations
  Diplomat, international body/organisation
- Being the only representative from your country
  Volunteer, charity worker
- Picking up work as you travel – blow your career
  Drifter

There is a huge difference working for an international organisation as opposed to a domestic one. In an international organisation, you'll be working with people of all nationalities from dawn to dusk. If you work for a large global company, you may have worldwide systems and procedures to follow which may be tiresome at times and frustrate you. Consider the impact your career choice will have on your lifestyle – it can make a big difference.

Strengthening your academic capabilities and looking at research

You may decide to focus on becoming a fully fledged scholar (some academics would argue that you are already), and remaining at university to pursue a career in research or lecturing. You may want to develop a very high level of knowledge, understanding and expertise in a particular part of the world, such as the Middle East, or focus on a global approach. Once you've made your choice, you'll need to consider how you want to apply and develop that knowledge, be it in academia, research institutes, the private sector or international organisations such as the UN. You can transfer this knowledge to industry and disseminate it through spin-out companies, created by universities as a result of new research.

There are currently over 20,000 people engaged in research in the UK alone. Many work on a project full time, or combine research with other responsibilities such as lecturing or clinical practice, often with others in the UK or abroad. Researchers are also often employed by research councils, the government and other relevant organisations to fulfil various responsibilities such as management, policy advice and project planning. As well as considering the usual academic routes, find out what bodies such as Regional Development Agencies (www.englandsrdas.com) are doing in your sector to support the movement of knowledge and ideas out of their scholarly world and into industry and commerce through the commercialisation of research into spin-out companies.

The Research Assessment exercise means that the higher education funding bodies can distribute funds for research on quality. Find out more by visiting www.rae.ac.uk for information on the Research Assessment Exercise 2008; and www.hero.ac.uk/rae. Ratings range from 1 to 5* and it gives an idea of the standard of UK research. See Further Reading and Useful Addresses at the end of this book. The normal route into research is to undertake a post-graduate course (see Chapter 3 for more information).

Keeping an interest in your degree

You may be feeling that you're not that bothered about using your languages at work. Perhaps you'll use your Russian to keep in touch your friends in Moscow, or your Spanish to email your mates in Madrid. Unless you make strident efforts to use your language and literature skills, they will dwindle fast and your brain will lose the mental and intellectual ability to pull on that rich vocabulary and fluency you acquired at university. To stop this happening, you could:

+ Become a tutor at an adult education centre. There are many courses run solely for the day designed to give people a taster or greater knowledge than they have already.
+ Tutor individuals on a one-to-one basis.
+ Continue to study for your own enjoyment, reading books around the subject and perhaps even starting up your own network of French/Mandarin/Russian speakers.
+ Take units at the local university or with the Institute of Linguists (see Useful Addresses at the end of this book).

What would be of key importance to you in your future career?

Identify the elements of work which are most important to you in your life and career such as those shown in Table 2.5. Which matter to you over any other, and do they reflect your own values? What does that tell you about your future career?

Moving your self-awareness forward

Your next step is to find out as much as you can about each industry to uncover the real range of employment opportunities within it. Find out what the pros and cons are – every industry has them – you need to know what you're letting yourself in for. The sector's professional body or trade association will be a good place to start. Chapter 4 will outline how such an organisation can help. Useful Addresses at the back of this book will direct you to places where you can access further information.

Once you have started to work out where you want to be and what you want to be doing, create your own goal, desired result – whatever you choose to call it and give it some focus and specifics. Life becomes easier. You're far more likely to achieve what you want if it reflects your values and excites you. Create a clear picture of what life will be like when you achieve your goal or target. Write your goal down as specifically as you can, to help you focus, and put it somewhere you can see it every day. Talk about what you do want to do – as opposed to what you don't – as if it were already

Table 2.5

Motivation	Work for me rather than anyone else
Use of language or linguistic skills	Results/outcomes
Purpose of work	Independence
Location	Entrepreneurship
Contribution to organisation/world/ sector/individuals	Personal fit – feeling that you belong? Skills you use
Sector – matching interests and knowledge	Values, as you identified in Chapter 1 Fit with lifestyle
Rules, ethics and behaviour	Knowledge you use
Role	Creativity
Rewards	Fun
Work–life balance	Using my degree subject to the full

happening. Give it a time limit, so that you have something to work for. Finally, make it sufficiently challenging to stretch you, but realistic. It will be more manageable if you break it down into bits, so that you can work out step-by-step what needs to be done when.

An example of a long-term career goal is:

In three years' time, I'll be:
➢ working for a publisher;
➢ paid off 40 per cent of my student debt;
➢ got a network of friends in London I feel I know really well.

In six months' time, I'll have:
➢ researched all the firms I want to apply to;
➢ found out what I need to do to qualify;
➢ made the necessary networking contacts;
➢ attended my first job interview.

Ask the right high quality questions and you're more likely to get high quality answers.

A word on family expectations

Families can play a key role in our future career planning, unfortunately sometimes to the detriment of our own judgement of what is right for us. *'I went into it to please my parents'*, often means that graduates went into safe, respectable careers which met with nods of approval and sighs of relief from their family, but made them, the graduate, feel they were en route to jail for a working lifetime.

Today, most families are more relaxed about career choice – *'You can't tell them – they make their own minds up!'* – frequently with all the inference that they still know better. They want us to be safe, protected, happy and successful and a misunderstanding of the job market and a tendency to take on board negative messages from the media makes things worse. There's nothing like the unknown and misunderstood to make people select the safe and known. While our friends and family have our interests very much at heart, their own agendas and self-interest and experiences may colour their well-meaning advice to us. They know our qualities well, but may have a limited experience and knowledge of the job market. Pin-point a couple of practical ways they could help so that at the least they feel as though they are doing something.

If your family and friends have not gone through the process of higher education and have been in lower-level jobs, seek to engage with people who are now in the career roles you aspire to, i.e. in the place where you want to be. Keep your sights high.

Summary action points

Bringing all the answers to the exercises in this chapter together.

1   What sort of a picture of your future career is emerging? What am I doing in it?
2   What information do I need to firm this picture up?
3   What do I need to happen next to help me further my career plans?
4   What do I need to know to start making decisions?

Chapter 3

Working out 'how to'

This chapter is all about the 'how'.

How will you get to where you want to be? What could you do to reach the outcome you want? What will you do to position yourself to be in a strong position to make the life you want happen?

Focusing your energies in the right direction with a plan will be a good start, because it will fill your life with vision, purpose and energy, and you'll waste less time on things which aren't important. You can consider all the different ways to get to where you want to be, and to position yourself to follow the best route to make it happen.

As you're deciding on your career, you need to take into account the financial aspect of it all as well and how you're going to start and make it happen. You may need to take a long-term five-year view to get to where you want to be, or you may get a break far faster than that simply through networking in the right places, winning a competition which brings your name to the forefront of the industry you want to be in, or hit on an idea which finds favour with an investor or two. Plot a strategy, and then position yourself to make sure it happens for you and that you tap the right sources of help along the way.

What could your next steps be?

Your next steps could involve all or any of the following, as shown in Figure 3.1.

The steps shown in Figure 3.1 may *all* feature at sometime in your working life, either alone or in combination. They may just appear as an opportunity too good to miss.

The next five steps for you to take are:

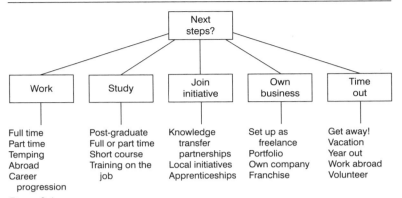

Figure 3.1

1   Be clear in your own mind what you want to do.
2   Look at how far you've got in making that happen.
3   Identify what you're missing in terms of skills, qualifications, knowledge and experience.
4   Decide on the best way to fill any gaps.
5   Get on and do it. While you're doing it, keep an eye on anything else you need to do to boost your chances of success in making your career and life goals happen.

This may take some time to work out. Networking will help, because you'll be able to talk to people who are already where you want to be, and ask them about the best way forward.

Side-stepping the career issue for a moment ...

While you're considering the above five steps, ask yourself:

*   Do you want to have a break from the serious side of life and do something wild and wacky for a few months, such as travelling or taking time out?
*   Is there anything else you would like to do for your own personal fulfilment and life journey, as opposed to for career reasons, such as studying a post-graduate course for the sheer joy of immersing yourself in a subject for a year or more?

If the answer to either of these is yes, then you will need to compare how important they are to you alongside everything else. It may be you can travel later, once your career is up and running, but more on that later.

Heading off out to work

Graduates have a wider choice of careers than ever before. This choice has been increasing in length and breadth over the decades, moving from a range of careers for which a degree was essential, such as teachers, medical sciences and veterinary science, to those areas where, increasingly, employers sought graduates as their first choice. Initially, this hit areas such as management, administrative posts in the public and private sector and IT, but recently degrees have been sought by new sectors. Examples include management accountancy, sales and marketing and buying and purchasing. Many of these have graduate trainee schemes. There are also increasingly the back office support roles in operations and compliance, administration and office management. This is especially so as executive assistants and personal assistants increasingly take on the work of junior and middle management.

In the newer areas where graduates are fairly recent, you will need to be particularly pro-active in ensuring that your career develops in the way you want it to. Chapters 6 and 9 go into this in more detail because there are a number of things you can do to help yourself. Entry to many of these areas is being smoothed over through initiatives created by government agencies, such as the Knowledge Transfer Partnerships, and structured internships and work experience placements. Such partnerships help knowledge and research developed by the universities to spread throughout industry. Students are literally passing on the knowledge they have acquired in their course. Check to see what your region is doing to help you make an entry.

Many graduates moving into work for which a degree is not required, such as retail, bar and restaurant work, and lower-level administrative roles, often do so simply to start work, or perhaps to save money to go travelling. Choose to take these roles and you will need to try that much harder to pull yourself out of them if you want to change career or progress. In addition, you won't enjoy the same salaries and perks those higher up the career ladder partake in. Consequently, dissatisfaction may rise to give thoughts such as *'Why did I go to university and land myself with such a debt?'* Strategic planning can help you work your way out of it, together with regular self-assessment, plotting, planning, monitoring and reviewing while everyone else parties and sleeps.

Get action planning if you want to go out to work in a 'graduate' job.

1   Recognise that the 'graduate' job has become much wider in scope than it used to be.
2   Be clear about the skills you want to use in it, as outlined in Chapter 2, such as research, analysing, your intellectual abilities, team leadership, risk taking, creative thinking etc.
3   Be hungry for the responsibilities which will come with it.
4   Make good use of graduate websites such as www.doctorjob.com and www.prospects.ac.uk to help you link into employers.
5   Be open to new possibilities such as the SME (small and medium enterprise) market and creating your own business.

What steps do you need to take to fulfil your long-term career and life goals?

One of the first things you need is a vision, especially if you're setting up your own business. Imagine filming yourself on video at work immediately after university. Then wind the film forward to three to five years' time. Where are you and what are you doing? Your answers will help you plot your path to success by breaking the longer period down into manageable chunks and tackle them one by one. It's easier to focus on where you're headed. Meantime, you need to bring the cash in.

Working while developing your own business or waiting to get into the line of work you really want to do

There are two choices here. You can temp or work part time or flexible hours for an employer.

People temp for many reasons. You could do it to give yourself time to decide what to do, using its flexibility to build your portfolio of work, making contacts, getting a foot in the door of the industry you want to work in. You can also use it to pick up lots of ideas for your own business, watching how businesses do things, considering how design can help companies grow or not and help people work more effectively together. It can be helpful to sharpen up your business skills and approach.

If you choose to temp through an agency, remember that they are businesses seeking to make a profit, so take responsibility for plotting and planning your own career. Keep your eye on your career and the goal you're aiming for. The *danger* of temping if you're using it as a 'way in' or deciding what to do with your life, is that you could still find yourself temping after a year, with no further progress in your decision making. Even temporary posts can form an important part of your career planning. When you're deciding which agencies to sign up with, look at their websites and track record. Who are their main clients? Do they appeal to you?

More employers are offering increasingly flexible opportunities and ways to work, such as a three-day week or a four-day week (ten hours over four days), or night working at an enhanced rate, leaving your days free (don't forget you need to catch up on your sleep). These may give you the assurance you need that the money is coming in leaving you free to focus on your goal in the holidays, weekends and any spare time you have.

Many people take any job going to bring some money in while they are working to establish themselves or get into the industry they really want to work in. It is not uncommon for people to have two or even three jobs at the same time. Temporary work at least offers flexibility but no guarantee of a regular income. The time you spend worrying about whether you'll have work next week may well be better devoted to your caeer planning. It will, however, put you right into the heart of the workplace, enabling you to build up a web of contacts around a number of companies. You'll quickly find that you're not the only one doing a day job and then getting home to focus on their main job. Many workers in the UK moonlight, doing their bread-and-butter job in the day, and work at something else more appealing at night. In many cases, these latter efforts will become full-time businesses. There is the opportunity to work at one thing while looking to achieve a long-term goal doing something totally different. This divided loyalty can create stresses and strains, as you leave your day job and then switch over when you get home to your own special aspirations and the reality of making them work for you. Focus will be the key to success, with lots of energy and a strong vision of where you're headed.

Don't lose your ambitions and aspirations while temping or working part time

1   Create a vision, a mission, a goal, perhaps a niche and be clear about what you want to do.
2   Break it down into manageable chunks, so that every time you achieve a chunk, you feel that you're really making progress to your overall goal.
3   Be prepared to consider routes which might not necessarily demand a degree.
4   Give yourself a timescale.
5   Ensure that you're giving this goal the prominence in your life that it truly deserves.
6   Be clear about how important it is to you.
7   Understand what it will cost you if you don't achieve it.

Going it alone

Running your own business or doing your own thing is about fulfilling your own dreams and not those of someone else. For many, working for someone else deadens their creativity, freedom, independence, fun, being able to work when you want at what you want. The good news is that there is more support and help out there than ever before, at a national and regional level. If you want to be a writer, for example, there's plenty of advice for you on rates to charge and business practical know-how on many writing sites. There is considerable help for start-ups, from innovative centres where you can hire an office and share facilities at inexpensive rates, to advice from business advisers, events and online sites designed to help you make all the right decisions. And make no mistake, however much you want to work at your craft, be it writing, training, teaching, translating, interpreting or whatever it is that you plan to do, you need to take a business approach.

Take advice: networking clubs can help you talk to fellow entrepreneurs and help each other. In September 2004, Chancellor Gordon Brown launched the National Council for Graduate Enterpreneurship. (www.ncge.org.uk). It in turn has set up Flying Start (www.flyingstart-ncge.com) and backed by One NorthEast, the area's regional development agency, and the bridge club, a company based in Newcastle-upon-Tyne which fosters enterprise.

Self-employment is not the rosy picture it often appears. Many small companies are being strangled by red tape and the compensation culture, and it can be a very lonely affair. Consider how you'll handle tasks such as planning the vision for your business, writing a business plan, setting yourself financial targets, dealing with health and safety issues, accounting and financial responsibilities, taking on staff and keeping to the right side of the law, keeping the books and records, on-going business development, product and service development, dealing with the taxman, accountant and suppliers. It could be that your degree course has prepared you well for this – all you need now is just the idea to set your business alight with activity!

You could become a portfolio worker, i.e. hold down two or more jobs, or set yourself up as a freelance, offering services and products by an hourly or daily rate. Alternatively, you could buy a franchise which is a tried and tested product, or set up a business selling products. The British Franchise Association (see Useful Addresses) is the only independent accreditation body for franchising in the UK. Franchises cover a wide range of areas from pet care to refill printer cartridges, accountancy and taxation services to training centres. There are also workshops and seminars to give you lots of advice and tips on choosing a franchise and running a successful business. Before you buy any franchise, check its financial status and insist on seeing the accounts from their head office. An example of a language-related franchise is La Jolie Ronde, http://www.lajolieronde.co.uk, which teaches French to children of pre-secondary school age.

Develop an idea, create a vision, do your homework and research the market thoroughly, and make your decision.

Consider the following questions:

- What do you want your business to achieve? What do you want it to do?
- What will it look like in five years' time?
- What financial targets will it meet in six months', one year, three years and five years?
- Who will your customers/clients be? Where will they come from?

- What will your unique selling points be? What niche do you intend to focus on?
- What position will you take in the market?
- What brand do you want? What values will your business portray?
- What will your reputation be based on?
- What message and language can you use to grab potential customers' attention?
- What story would a SWOT analysis give you? How does that compare with your competitors in the market?
- What can you do to give your product or service that extra special added value, or to please and surprise your customer or client?
- Where will you run the business from?
- How will running a business impact on your lifestyle?

There will also be key operational questions to consider such as:

- What funding do you need right now to set up and give yourself an income?
- How will you structure the business (e.g. limited company, sole trader, partnership)?
- How will you market your products and services?
- How will you price your products and services?
- What equipment will you need to get started?
- How soon can you get up and running?

If you don't know how to go about any of these things, remember that university has given you the ability *to find them out*. When you started university, you asked where things were, who you needed to talk to in order to get a, b and c done. You knew nothing about the place when you started but you quickly learnt the ropes and found out what you needed to know to make the most of your university days. You can do this again.

You could also provide a freelance service to companies and organisations which saves them taking you on and gives you more flexibility. You simply invoice those who have bought your service at the end of each month or piece of work with your fee. Agree how any expenses are to be covered right from the start – don't assume that they will be, and bear in mind that some companies have their own policies as to what they will reimburse and what they won't.

Time management and the ability to change focus will be essential if you want to work on a full- or part-time basis while establishing yourself

You need to be very disciplined and swift to adapt from the day job to your real passion, and not waste any time slumping in front of the television for a 30-minute break which can then last the entire evening. A sharp 30–40 minutes' exercise, meditation or yoga can do wonders for clearing and re-energising your mind, soul and body before you switch from one job to the other. Find a pattern which works for you. If you work well in the morning, do a couple of hours while the rest of the country sleeps and then go out to the day job knowing you've already made headway in your real job. It makes you feel positive. Do some work every single day – never leave it, because once you do so once, you're more likely to do it for two or three days on the trot, and then you lose the momentum.

What further learning do you need to undertake?

Closing that gap between where you are now and where you want to be

There are many learning opportunities which will enable you to close that gap, including:

- Informal course run by a university on interview techniques, writing a CV, tackling assessment centres.
- A (postgraduate) qualification to equip you for the career you have in mind, such a teaching, translating, interpreting, publishing. There are post-graduate qualifications in all these subjects.
- A short course to help you set up your own business delivered through agencies such as your local Business Link or college, covering areas such as business functions, customer care, marketing and selling, health and safety issues, and motivating people.
- A Masters degree in Research if you're looking to proceed up the academic ladder to lecturing and research or a course with a strong research element.

- A short course in a specific area such as Teaching English as a Second Language which will give you a fast route into employment.
- Boosting your knowledge and understanding of a particular sector, if you want to work and specialise in it.

There are various forms of learning: informal, where you find the information you need to mug up on and learn about it yourself; and the more formal, set in short or longer courses. Identify what you need to know or have expertise in to be successful in the work you want to do, find out where you can get this learning and what you need to apply for it (resources, financial, knowledge, talent etc.) and then do it.

To be ... a post-graduate or not?

If you need or want to take your knowledge and skill expertise to another level, you could enrol on a post-graduate course such as:

- Career entry related courses, for which you need no experience, such as the Post Graduate Certificate in Education (PGCE).
- A course that will enhance your career progression, such as the MBA – usually for those who already have a couple of years' relevant work experience.
- Research-based studies, such as the PhD (Doctor of Philosophy), which take about three or four years full time to complete and which can take you into the field of research.
- A post-graduate degree which is taught, or which is taught and involves research. Business-related subjects include management, marketing, human resources, finance, banking, accounting and recreational management. Ask yourself if you would be better suited studying for a professional qualification. Weigh up your options and talk to professionals in the field before you decide what to do.
- A post-graduate course which takes you into a specific niche such as the Postgraduate Certificate for Interpreter Trainers.

Some employers sponsor employees through degree and post-graduate courses and may even approach a university to create a bespoke course and qualification for their employees. Equally, some people study a post-graduate degree for their own (career) development, perhaps part time or online. People study post-graduate degrees for various reasons, to boost their career prospects or to simply increase their specialist knowledge and expertise in a particular area. Many students work for several years before taking a full-time post-graduate degree. By this time, they can envisage exactly how that study will fit into longer-term career plans, plus they've got experience to talk about when they finally come to getting that post-graduate job. Timing is tricky: leave it too long and it may be too late to put impetus and fresh energy into your career.

Questions to ask before you sign up for a post-graduate degree

1   How does this course take you closer to achieving your long-term career plans? Where does it fit within them?

2   Will a post-graduate degree substantially boost your chances of success? Will it really give you that edge over your competitors? What do employers think?

3   Are you simply contemplating post-graduate study simply to put off joining the working world for another year? (The longer you leave it, the harder it may be.)

4   What are the costs and what funding is available?

5   What have post-graduate students gone on to do after their studies? How do these paths relate to your aspirations?

6   What will it take to be a successful applicant and student?

7   What are your motivations for taking such a course (e.g. entry into a new career, career progression)?

8   What can you do to sell the benefits of a post-graduate degree to an employer? Many employers have enough problems understanding the benefits of an undergraduate degree, never mind the focus, rigour and academic discipline required to do a post-graduate one.

9   Is it really a post-graduate course you need, or would another form of study and learning be more appropriate for the skills and knowledge you seek? Get specific advice about your learning needs.

What evidence do you have that post-graduate study will enhance your employment prospects? Could networking and getting the right experience under your belt, perhaps by doing an internship, be as effective?

Further information on post-graduate studies

You'll find the official UK post-graduate database at www.prospects. ac.uk which lists the different courses available by subject, region and institution in the UK. You can apply online through Prospects. In the UK, apply as soon as you can because the more popular courses fill up quickly – this means often October or November in the year before the course is due to start. The National Postgraduate Committee (www.npc.org.uk) represents the interests of post-graduate students in the UK, so make good use of it.

If you live outside the UK, the British Council (www.britcoun. org) has offices throughout the world and can give you lots of information about studying and living in Britain. NARIC (the National Academic Recognition Information Centre, www.naric.org.uk) provides a service for international students who want information on the comparability between international and UK qualifications.

Short courses may be just the ticket

A short course may boost your employability and give you the skills you need to get that post you want. In the UK, you can find these at www.hotcourses.com. You could also visit your local college and private training companies to find out what they have to offer. A short course or workshop may also provide you with just the springboard you need to bounce into a new career. An example is Scriptnaked, which offers courses and workshops and professional development opportunities for aspiring and practising screenwriters. The Diploma in Public Service Interpreting or the Diploma in Translation, both run at Middlesex University are examples of short course qualifications. The former qualification would enable you to join the National Register of Public Service Interpreters.

Courses should be very practical to give you confidence and practice, and the course tutors should also have strong and current contacts with employers in the sector. A career development loan (www.direct.gov.uk/cdl) may be last thing you feel like acquiring but, if you live in the EU, it could just provide you with the finance you need to fill that vocational skill gap and boost your employability.

Some tests are set by the employer or with him in conjunction with another body to prepare students for a specific career with that organisation. An example is the Metropolitan Police Test, which has an Oral Test, involving consecutive interpreting and consecutive interpreting of a statement, and a written part, with a technical translation. If you choose to go into any niche area, you need to familiarise yourself with the technology used in the sector and you can do this by informal learning, such as reading, work shadowing and studying sample papers. See Useful Addresses at the end of this book for more information.

In the UK, Language Services Ltd can assess your skills in a number of languages.

Short on skills and business knowledge?

A combination of subjects taken at university may have given you skills and knowledge in areas such as business studies, administration, marketing and public relations. You may need to pick these up through short courses on offer locally. LearnDirect (www.learn-direct.co.uk offers such courses to small companies. ACAS (www.acas.org.uk) covers the human resources side of things and it's worth taking some of their courses if you plan on recruiting staff in the UK – they are extremely cost effective.

Equally, you can pick up a lot from work experience and temping – how businesses function, ways in which you can carry out the normal business functions such as administration, book-keeping, record-keeping, invoicing, health and safety, communicating with employees. It will also teach you how the business world works and behaves, and you can learn to speak the corporate lingo so that you better understand potential clients.

Enrolling for professional qualifications

You may plan to study for professional qualifications once you have decided on the business function you wish to work with. These give you the core knowledge and competences which you need to perform effectively at work; they give you the theory and practice which gives you a competitive edge. In some industries, you cannot advise clients or practice without them. Working towards them normally involves taking a number of examinations and practical experience. Consider which is best for you. Think about how you want to study, be it online, by evening class, through block learning or distance learning. Professional bodies will have a list of accredited training providers and most have a very considerable range of support mechanisms to help you through. If you want to study for a qualification out of your home country, check to see how it would be viewed if you suddenly came home.

Study part time while working?

Look back to the reasons why you enrolled for an undergraduate or post-graduate degree. Perhaps you did so with your employer's knowledge, blessing and support. If this is the case, discuss your future with your employer, your direct boss or HR or both.

Questions to consider

- What do I want to happen next?
- How can I use my new-found knowledge and skills to boost my personal effectiveness now and to prepare me for the next stage in my career?
- Where do I see my career going in the next five years? How has this goal changed since starting my studies?
- What do I need to do now to make this happen?
- How has my new degree status changed my CV and what I have to offer?
- If I were to re-write my CV for my next perfect role, what would be missing from where I am now and that new description? How likely is it that I can make that happen at my current company?
- How do I see myself doing this: with my current employer, with another employer or starting up alone?

Whatever you choose to do, stretch your new confidence and intellectual prowess. Work to achieve your potential, not to reduce it because your current role isn't right for you. That may mean cutting the strings with your current employer.

'I want to work abroad!'

There's no doubt working abroad gives you a tremendously different outlook to those who have not been so fortunate to experience such an opportunity. Recruitment companies who have an international reach often have advice on their sites about moving abroad. For example, www.asia.hobsons.com has information on working in China, Taiwan, Thailand, Hong Kong, Singapore, Malaysia, Indonesia and Japan with market trends and industry summaries, and overall regional outlooks plus details of events in the area. Prospects (www.prospects.ac.uk) has numerous country profiles, incorporating details of the job market, international companies in the region you're reading about, language requirements, work experience, vacancy sources and visa and immigration information. Working abroad requires considerable research and preparation if you're to have the experience you want – they all vary greatly. Further Reading at the end of this book has useful suggestions.

Questions to consider

1   What do you want to get out of the experience?
2   Where do you want to work? Do you want to take the opportunity to learn a new language or improve existing language skills?
3   What do you want to do? Do you want to work for an employer in a job which will contribute to your career progression or simply go apple picking for six months?
4   How different do you want the culture of the country you're going to be working in to be from your own?
5   How will your current qualifications be regarded in the country you plan to work in – will you need to get any additional 'top up' qualifications to meet their own regulations and criteria to work as a practising professional?
6   What visa requirements will there be? What happens about health insurance? What are the tax implications for you while working abroad and when you return home?
7   Can you do it under the auspices of your current or a future employer?
8   How long do you want to do it for?

Time out for golden sands, sea, sun ...

If you've been on the academic treadmill all your life without a break, you may feel that it's time for some time out, fun and rest. Increasing numbers of people of all ages are taking time out and more (larger) employers are offering employees sabbaticals. They like seeing them return to the workplace refreshed, with a new confidence, fresh ideas, great soft skills and creativity. Gap programmes too are waking up to the fact that more of us want time out, and provide excellent opportunities for voluntary work and travel.

That said, you live your life once. The moment you stop experiencing such adventures as travel and facing challenges in life, you stop living and start existing. If you plan to take some time out, you could look for a job before you go and try to negotiate a start date for when you return (assuming you will return); or you could travel and look for a job when you get back. This gives you more flexibility and possibly more stress as you wonder how on earth you're going to find a job and pay off your debts when you get home.

Unemployment ...

Not a very inspiring option, is it? So get busy.

Seven ways to pass the time while you're unemployed

1   Get relevant work experience, even if it's just for a week or a couple of days a week over a month or so.
2   Do voluntary work.
3   Learn new skills.
4   Travel.
5   Job hunt persistently and seriously.
6   Do something quite mad and quirky to make your CV stand out.
7   Study for a qualification which will give you on-the-job skills.

Acknowledge that this is a difficult time, because you've been through all the hard work towards your graduation, celebrated in style, promised complete strangers you met in the Union Bar in the last 24 hours at university that you'll keep in touch ... and suddenly, it's all over. And it's a strange feeling, so acknowledge it and then turn your attention to the future.

Give your life a turbo-boost!

If you're currently sitting at home aimlessly with no defined plans or goals and no meaningful way to fill your day, it's time to change that. Climb out of where you are now and start walking purposefully to where you want to be.

1   Make use of the careers support in your area.
2   Search out professional organisations which can help you build networks leading to introductions in the sectors you need.
3   Talk to fellow graduates. What sort of business could you start up together based on your mutual interests and passions?
4   Build up a clear picture of the sector you wish to go into and be clear about how your skills, strengths and interests will contribute to it.
5   Talk to as many people as you can by going to where you know you'll find them outside the usual graduate arena, such as trade exhibitions, local networking events.
6   Brainstorm strategies you can use which will boost your chances of success, such as a willingness to move and live where the sector is strongest geographically.
7   Find out what is going on to encourage graduates to work for small and medium-sized companies.
8   Set yourself daily targets and goals in every area of your life, not just your career. Life isn't just about work.

Summary action points

Move your thinking forward:

1   Who do I need to talk to in order to find out which entry routes are available to me?
2   What do I need more of in my life? How can I get it?
3   What steps will I take next and how will they move me closer to my goals? What do I need to do to make them happen?
4   Which university or college runs the course in the subject I'm looking for?
5   What funding is available for me to set up my own business?
6   What initiatives are available that might be relevant to me and my career goals?

Chapter 4

Connecting with your network

The world's a network

Connecting to those in the know who can help you move closer to the things you want in life will enable you to enjoy a far richer life and career. Chapters 4 and 5 will help you pinpoint people who can help you create or open doors to new opportunities.

A strong, active network can open doors to decision makers and in turn enable you to reach out, help others and live a highly successful and fulfilling life. Whatever stage of life and career you are at, it will enhance your prospects of obtaining the introductions you need. Highly successful people have a network of business associates, acquaintances colleagues and friends they can turn to for information, advice, introductions and help. You create your own luck and networks in life, however, and they are as active and useful and productive as you make them. Remember that networking is also about helping those who *have* helped you, and those who *haven't*.

This chapter considers the *Who* question in a networking capacity.

- *Who* can help me?
- *Who* can give me the support I need now?
- *Which* websites will be most useful?

Eight steps to successful networking

1   An ability to chat and be really interested in the other person; you need to be able to establish a rapport with strangers quickly.
2   Listening and questioning skills.
3   A get-up-and-go attitude – go out there and fight for your place in the world.

4   Follow through. Use the information you acquire, file it for future thought, action it or dump it, but *do* something with it.
5   Lateral thinking – does your contact know of anyone else you should talk to?
6   Respect! The person you're talking to has got to where they are by hard work. They believe in what they are doing and in what the job stands for. It may not turn out to be your niche or world, but respect them for what they love about theirs.
7   Be inquisitive and curious.
8   Accept feedback calmly.

You may not always like what you hear. Challenge the person giving feedback politely. *'This is a very tough industry and not many people make it to the starting blocks.'* Okay, so that may be the case, but clearly people *do* need to make it so you need to focus on that percentage – whatever it is – the 5, 10, 20 per cent of applicants – and find out just what it is that brings them success. Focus on the people who've succeeded, not on generalisations that *'It's difficult, it's tough.'* It may well be, but it's not impossible. Turn the negatives around to: *'It's difficult, but it's possible. It's tough but it's rewarding.'* Talk about the *'I can'* and *'I will'* rather than the *'I'll try'* or *'Maybe …'*. Ask people *'What is your perception of me?'* to get feedback on how you present yourself and how you come over. This will help give them something to remember you by. *'I met with a journalist who was absolutely passionate about … really great ideas and done some terrific projects. You should give them a call – might be able to help you …'*.

What would be the cost to you if you *didn't* achieve your career goals? Envisaging such an outcome can provide a terrific leverage to get you out of your comfort zone and make those phone calls and send the emails to make contacts. It can propel you into making that extra effort, going the extra mile and turning the last corner to find the right opening. What are you prepared to do in order to make sure it happens? How outlandish are you prepared to be in the way you tackle a situation, and how far out of your comfort zone are you prepared to go to make it happen? Your passion for your career and what you want to achieve should inspire and excite you so much that you're prepared to do what it takes to sell yourself. True networking is only really effective when you push yourself out of your comfort zone and think out of the box.

A key benefit to your networking activities will be to create and build a strong support team around you. Each person on your team should bring you something different. There will be members of your support team you've known all your life, such as your family, family friends and your friends. Within that group, there will be one or two people whom you trust perhaps just that little bit more than the rest. You know they will be open and honest with you and you also know you can handle any constructive criticism from them because it's fair and just. Then there are people who fill you with energy, a 'can do' approach, who could inspire you to great things. Perhaps these may include your peers at university; how often have you sat about and brainstormed an idea late into the night which is going to make you all lots of money and bring you fame? Keep in regular contact with those friends who enable you to unlock your potential and your creativity. There will also be the people you (secretly) admire and consider your success and role models. They may be a member of your family, perhaps your mother or father; or they could be a high profile leader in business, politics, the community, or someone with a 'go ahead' approach which fills you with energy and passion for your own beliefs and causes. Bring these people on board by studying their methods to achieve success. What did they sacrifice along the way to get to where they wanted to be? How did they focus? Why not contact them to ask them how they did it and what advice they have for you? Would they even act as a mentor to you? Finally, there are those who are not yet known to you – those people working in the sort of profession you want to be in, those who can advise you and help you along the way. It is here that the skill of networking truly comes into its own.

The benefits of networking

Networking is all about asking others to help you access information which will help you – or others – get to where you need to be. You can access information and decision makers. You can tap into those in the know who are most likely to know the answer you need – it's a bit like the 'phone a friend' lifeline on the UK television programme *Who Wants to be a Millionaire?* The contestants choose the friend who is mostly likely to know the answer to the question they are faced with, and it's the same here. You need to reach those beyond those you know and extend a line and call for information and help to those you *don't*.

This is the same in life. We all need the right people to call on in moments of crisis because we know they will give us the right support at that moment. We choose our friends because they have qualities we admire and enjoy. We elect to take some family members into our confidence as opposed to others because we know they have something slightly different to offer us, perhaps due to their life experience or their approach or attitude. As we go through life, we'll call on people at different times and there will be periods when we aren't in touch at all. Nonetheless, keep those fires of warmth and support burning because we know that when the time comes, we'll need to know we can pick up the telephone and call them or drop them an email to ask for help, even if it's just a friendly ear. Just the same way, there are people who know they can call on us.

Let's consider how networking can help you in your career. If you brainstorm all the people you know, who you've met or watched at presentations as they came into your university, you can probably draw up a long list of names, as shown in Figure 4.1.

Fifteen ways networking can help you in your career

1   Acquiring relevant work experience, especially in highly competitive sectors where contacts are everything.
2   Help with your CV, application or portfolio.
3   Information about a career or organisation, or better still, an introduction to someone working in it.
4   An idea of the skills, qualities and experience an employer wants and the personalities they recruit; would you be a good 'fit'?
5   How a sector works, e.g. the culture, behaviour, dress, language, values.
6   The name of the best recruitment agency for you to talk to.
7   Advice on the best way 'in' to a sector or company.
8   Projects an employer needs doing but does not have the resource internally to undertake which you could then volunteer for.
9   Tip-offs when a job comes up – many companies advertise their vacancies to staff first on their notice boards or company intranet.
10   Finding out what roles are available for new graduates.
11   Discovering the best place to look for vacancies.

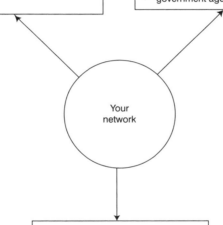

In the sector you want to work in:

- within a company
- across different companies in the sector
- universities to find out what's new and hot on the knowledge front
- university to university, if you're an academic
- professional bodies
- organisations devoted to the sector e.g. National Centre for Languages
- cluster groups, on a national, regional and local basis
- graduate initiatives, e.g. Knowledge Transfer Partnership
- links between universities and employers

Networks dedicated to start-up businesses or helping graduates:

- the self-employed and small business networks such as the Federation of Small Businesses
- government bodies, e.g. BusinessLink
- cross-cultural networks and organisations
- organisations targeted at particular groups, e.g. Women In Rural Enterprises
- sector specific networks
- government agencies

Your network

Personal networks:

- leisure and hobby interests
- voluntary and public sectors
- community service organisations, e.g. Soroptimists (women) and Rotary International
- friends and family
- professionals, e.g. doctors, dentists
- product and service providers you use, e.g. banks, builders, garages, etc.
- school, college, university
- religious organisations
- fellow students – could you do something together?

Figure 4.1

12   Discussing the industry overall, its strengths, weaknesses, op-
      portunities and threats; the pros and cons of working in it and
      how it is structured.
13   Advice from small business owners as they reflect back on their
      own experiences of setting up. Did they make any mistakes
      they would warn others about?
14   Acquiring names of bodies and groups who are really helpful
      when setting up a business.
15   Learning names of grants or funding you can tap into.

Many people don't push their network into unknown areas so
never truly reap the benefits networking can bring.

The danger of networking with fellow graduates is that if you're
both in the same boat, you may simply spend time and energy be-
moaning the current state you're in, which won't change anything.
So if you're talking to a fellow graduate, have a good moan for five
minutes and then spend 15 minutes brainstorming in which you can
both change the situation you're in for the better and bounce ideas
and contacts off each other. One of those ideas could be the breakthrough you've been looking for (see Figure 4.2).

Get pushy and politely ask for help – most people will be delighted to help you

Six steps to pro-active networking

1   Identify what you need to know or what sort of people you
     want to meet and why they are important to you.
2   Identify the people you *do know* and imagine on paper what
     their network would be like.
3   Make contact and ask for advice and help. If someone has
     referred you to a contact, mention their name.
4   Approach people you don't know but can find more easily
     through relevant professional organisations and trade associa-
     tions.
5   Think big and laterally and you could connect to thousands of
     people worldwide at a stroke. The key is to secure introduc-
     tions to the people in the right place.
6   Be open to asking for advice and help.

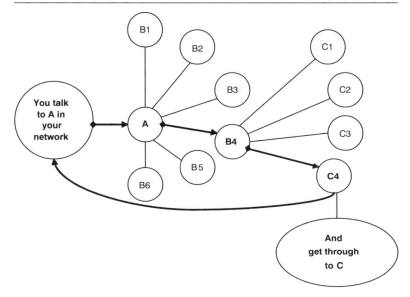

Figure 4.2

Professional organisations

Professional bodies exist partly to help promote the public's confidence in the professions they represent. As such, membership of a professional body may be essential to practice. They also help members and new entrants into the field to have satisfying and fulfilling careers, access to the right training and networks, and meet the challenges and opportunities that come their way. Many such organisations in the creative industries are listed under Useful Addresses at the back of this book. They will have advice for you, the new entrant, the career changer, the mature student, the young professional. They can point you towards areas of their website which may be particularly relevant to you. This book lists those relating to language and literature careers, but you can pick up many more from www.worktrain.org.uk and www.prospects.ac.uk. Their sites may cover such topics as shown in Table 4.1.

Most professional bodies are sympathetic to the job seeker, especially those from college or university, or returning to work. On initial contact, you may talk to a person employed by the professional body to be at the end of the phone, offering information and advice. They will have particular hints and advice for you, the new

Table 4.1

• A register of practitioners and their areas of expertise and specialism, often with their contact details	• Career case studies
	• Technical articles
	• Useful links
	• Information about the profession as a whole
• Events taking place at which members, associates and affiliates may gather	• Library services
	• Annual conferences in the UK and abroad
• Jobs search	• Salary calculator
• Online forum groups	• Services available to the public
• Latest industry news	• Vacancy listings
• Latest publications relevant to the industry	• Advice line on pricing issues
	• Setting up on your own
• Research	
• Information for the public on the body, its standards, ethics and training	

entrant, the career changer, the mature student, the young professional. They can also help point you in the direction of areas of their website which may be of interest and to local groups in your area.

For example, visit the websites for and make contact with the Institute of Linguists, the Institute of Translators and Interpreting – you will find them listed under Useful Addresses. Many professional organisations or websites have registers of professionals offering varying services such as translators and interpreters. BLIS Professionals is one of these, and you may want to consider signing up with them when you're ready to launch your services. Membership may be essential if you're to practice as a professional. If you're considering joining a profession, find your way around its website.

Much depends, however, on the professional body and you can get an idea for what they are like by talking to members and others involved in the sector. The Institute of Linguists is a professional body of highly qualified linguists and it has various membership divisions for areas such as translators, interpreters, language teachers, academics and language trainers. The Educational Trust provides language exams and operates the National Register of Public Service Interpreters. This covers professional interpreting for local government, health care and legal agencies so if you are a qualified interpreter speaking one of the many languages in the community, there may be opportunities for you to earn money here.

Many professional bodies are allied to international groups, thereby giving them a global view and contacts. In time, you may want to consider whether you want to join these – it could be a fabulous way to expand your network, in the European Union or further afield. Many organisations promote the benefits of their sectors to citizens through events, such as the European Day of Languages, conceived by the Council of Europe. Your company could play a local role in promoting these in partnership with a local college and enhance its profile and image in the local community accordingly. The *Association Internationale des Interpretes de Conference (AIIC)* is an international association of conference organisers and the UK has its own AIIC representatives.

Professional bodies' discussion forums are very useful to see what the hot topics are and to be able to comment on them at interviews or assessment days. It is not uncommon for people to ask for careers advice and point out that they are looking to move into an area, and for other professionals to come forth with advice and information. Many organisations have local networks, with regular meetings (sometimes with a speaker), events, training programmes and newsletters. There may also be visits to businesses for a look around, or a social gathering. Most will enable members to talk to each other and catch up, meet new people or give each other referrals.

Go on – attend a meeting in your area

It is in the organisation's vested interests to show you goodwill and interest and yours to represent yourself in a professional manner. Dress in business attire – suit and tie – and practice good social skills – a warm, firm handshake, a smile and lots of eye contact. Ask questions – what do people do, who do they work for, what sort of clients do they have. If they give you their business card, follow it up with an email saying something like 'It was nice to meet you – would it possible for us to meet up? – I'd love to talk you further about …'. Be ready to talk positively about your course, the projects you did and that you are currently working on, your career plans and people who inspire you. Mention articles you've seen in the press or online which show you're up-to-date and show enthusiasm and interest. Find out before you go about any initiatives in your area which are running to strengthen the relationship between graduates and small employers – it could just help swing the mind of a small employer to give a graduate like you a chance, if only he or she had some guidance on how to make the most of you.

If the thought of attending such a meeting fills you with horror...

Why not contact the person in charge of your local group to explain that you're coming along for the first time and to ask for someone to look out for when you arrive to introduce yourself to? There should be someone there whose role it is to welcome new members and make them feel at home. Look out for them and ask them to introduce you to someone who is working in a specific area that you'd like to get involved with. Find out in advance who will be there, and head for those you most want to talk to when you arrive, armed with prepared questions. Be interested and you'll soon forget your own nerves. Remember that you're with a group of like-minded people who may well remember what it's like to start out. They're on your side. Ask to meet them to find out more. Identify specific questions to ask before you go so that it is clear you have given the meeting some thought and prepared well for it.

Join your alumni

Do it now; you'll find details on your university's website. Try tracking down past alumni who are working in sectors you want to join. They can answer many of your questions, give you advice and may be able to point you in the right direction for more help and support. Find out what they like and dislike about what they're doing, and what they see the challenges are from the point of view of their career and life. What appealed to them about the organisation they joined and how has the partnership fared so far? Where do they see it going in the future? Why not set up an e-group (you can do this through *Yahoo*, for example) of your fellow graduates to act as a focal point of ideas, contacts, support, advice and help?

Academic groups

Academics network across the world as much as professionals in the business field. They attend conferences, listen to papers, give presentations, undertake joint research projects, compare notes, research, debate, argue, discuss, discover and invent. They talk on the phone, they email and they have their own networks across their universities, research institutes and other relevant organisations. They live and breathe their subjects, and they're encouraged to work with business, whether they like it or not, and to create a far more entrepreneurial spirit in their departments and students.

You may be thinking that academic life is for you. Visit websites such as www.jobs.ac.uk for information on jobs in the higher education sector and check their institutions' own websites for vacancies. As well as academic posts, universities also need staff in areas such as finance, marketing, public relations, administration, student support, human resources and facilities and building management.

There are also university networks, such as:

* Association of University Language Centres (www.aulc.org);
* Subject Centre for Languages, Linguistics and Area Studies (www.llas.ac.uk);
* University Council of Modern Languages (UCML) (www.ucml.org.uk/).

Informal networks

As important as their formal peers, informal networks are the places to go to meet like-minded people who will cheer you up when you feel low, give you good, sound advice over a pint and talk about *the* latest design from the sector which is truly giving everyone the '*Wow!*' factor. You may find these networks in coffee houses, bars, restaurants, pubs – any place where people in the sector hang out. You can also tap into informal networks through any social situation; remember that talking to an accountant over a drink, he may have clients in the sector who just could provide that right introduction for you. Be chatty and interested, passionate and enthusiastic, keen and self-motivated and you'll attract help and support, but remember that you may need to go out of your way to find it.

What about websites?

You can access careers advice and information online and in person through a number of sites (see Useful Addresses at the end of this book); through university careers services and government providers; plus sites such as www.prospects.ac.uk and www.hobsons.com. Wherever you are, visit or contact your local university's careers service and find out what help is available to you as a new graduate. Be specific about the help you need. Know the questions you want answers to. Go into careers interviews knowing what you want to cover. Be honest with yourself and others – this is not a test. In addition, there may be sites geared towards graduates in your particular region, such as GradSouthWest (www.gradsouthwest.com) in the southwest of the UK (see Useful Addresses at the back of this book).

Sector specific

Websites in themselves can be invaluable, particularly if you use them to signpost you in the direction of other sites. There are also different levels of websites which can help you. It's worth checking national government websites to see what initiatives there are to encourage training in the skills you have – you may be able to offer your services and tap into them. For example, check out www. futureskillsscotland.org.uk and www.futureskillswales.com. Enterprise agencies in the area may also have advice for those starting out, details of trade shows, training, events, help-lines, agencies and links. Then there are the Regional Language Networks www.cilt. org.uk/rln/index.htm which are working to raise awareness of the value of languages for employability and also a whole plethora of professional bodies which are listed under Useful Addresses at the back of this book.

The Institute of Translation and Interpreting has regional, language and subject networks, which give you the chance to meet others in the field. If you are working in such an area, it is always useful to be able to give potential clients names and addresses of those who can cater for a specific sector, for example, someone who is a translator from Polish to English, which you know you cannot cover. It shows that you are well connected in the sector. In addition, if you have a family emergency or health issue which suddenly means you have to re-arrange your work, it can be helpful to form strategic alliances with others in the sector whom you can work with in such eventualities.

Regional networks are growing in all sorts of careers. Take writing, for example, www.newwritingnorth.com in the North East of England seeks to help new writing in all genres flourish and develop. Many have events, projects, events, careers advice and development sections on their websites. In turn, they link to other groups related to theirs, such as www.literaturenortheast.co.uk/ which lists events and readings and lots more in the region including http://www.new-playsnw.com/, NorthWest Playwrites. There will be writers circles, professional development networks, mentors, readers, social events, tips and tricks – all sorts of things, so do have a look. The BBC's Writers Room (www.bbc.co.uk/writersroom) has lots of useful links and you should follow them through to the various sites because you really will unearth a goldmine of information.

Start-ups

There are also websites for the small businesses and start-ups, such as the Federation of Small Businesses (www.fsb.org.uk) , the Small Business Service, Start-Ups and BusinessLink. They can all signpost you in the right direction. These will enable you to make friends and potential clients, customers or employers over the Internet. Again, some are very specific, such as Women in Rural Enterprises (WIRE) in the UK (see www.wireuk.org). Think laterally.

Networking outside your sector

This is important if you wish to gain new clients. If you're running a small business or freelance service, you need to decide how to pro-mote your services. In this instance, you could consider attending local events put on to help business people network and exchange business cards so that they can pick up on each other's services and how they may help businesses. Local networking events targeting small businesses may help. Explore the networks in your area and on the Internet, and assess which ones will be most appropriate to you.

Successful networking

Open-mindedness and generosity is crucial, but be discerning too. Listen to what people have to say, and then assess the information and feedback you're getting against what's important to *you* and your criteria.

Ten more steps to successful networking

1 Don't assume the information you're getting is current. Don't assume those you're talking to are up-to-date. Go that extra mile to check with the professional bodies and trade associa-tions.

2   Guard your safety. If you're meeting someone, do so in a public place or in their office premises. Visit the company's website to make sure their address is valid. Don't give too many personal details out over the Internet or telephone.

3   Present yourself to the highest standard possible using business behaviour and language. Dress in your interview suit then examine your image from head to toe in front of a long mirror at home. If you're self-employed, think about the image you want to portray about your business.

4   Use networking to digest strategies which will put you ahead of the competition, whether you're looking for a new job or starting and developing your own business.

5   Networking is a two-way process. When people help you, see if there is anything you can do to help them. Build on the relationships you develop. Treat others as you would like to be treated yourself.

6   If you are at a networking event, spend about five minutes talking to the person you're with and then move on. You are *all* there to meet as many people as possible, so close the conversation, *'It's been nice to meet you. Shall we exchange cards and move on?'*

7   What perception do you want the people you meet to have of you? Do you want to come over as someone who takes their career and chosen field seriously and passionately, or as someone who's out to have a good time? Are you portraying yourself to be someone who can be trusted and loyal?

8   Don't give the impression that you hop from one company to another. It costs employers money to recruit staff and they won't be too impressed if you arrive, work for a year or so, and then move. Word gets around, especially if you live in a small community or work in a small sector. Be discreet if you're looking elsewhere for opportunities.

9   Set yourself goals for each networking opportunity. What do you want to achieve from it? Divide your networks in groups and give each group a goal for the week or month. Measure your success. What are you doing that is yielding the best results?

10   Keep in touch with people in your network. Email them from time to time to ask how they are and how things are going. A network is only as active and alive as you make it.

Business coaches

Career and business coaches help you identify what is important to you, what you want to achieve and what you need to do to make that happen. Some coaches work in a niche, for example, only with small creative companies and individuals to help them achieve their business and personal goals. Check that your coach is qualified and trained and find out what experience he or she has before parting with any money.

Go out there and immerse yourself in the fabric and make-up of those working in the sector you want to get into

Aim to build up a very strong understanding of the world you want to work in and seek to identify who really knows the local scene and has an influence in it. Informal networks are as important as those which are of a professional foundation, so find out where people meet in your sector if you're in a new town and head on down there. It's a great chance to meet with like-minded people who share the same passions you do and they will pull you up when you're feeling low and point you in the direction of all sorts of useful resources.

Networking is for life!

Networking can be very helpful in all sorts of ways including:

1 finding specialist expert health advice;
2 locating the estate agent who will really get your house sold fast and is always the first to hear of houses coming onto the market;
3 getting your children into the right school;
4 looking after ageing relatives and making the system work to your advantage;
5 volunteering to give something back;
6 meeting people of like mind, such as knowing where the places are to go to meet fellow artists and designers;
7 asking about hotels for that special holiday next year;
8 meeting new people at the pub, in the gym and through your interests;

9   learning something new and keeping your life fresh and active;

10   having fun and giving something back at the same time.

Summary action points

The way you network at every level can affect the flavour and fabric in your life so make it a priority.

1   What network groups are there in your area which you can make contact with and get involved with? List them and make that first contact.

2   Find out if they have mentors to help people like yourself who want to get into the sector. If they do, ask if you can be allocated one.

3   Contact five people in your network. Ask if they know of anyone who could help you. Arrange to meet for a coffee to catch up with them or organise an information meeting.

Chapter 5

Hunting out the right opportunity

So far, you've ascertained what you want to do – now you need to work out how and where you want to do it.

How important is the 'where?' to you?

What factors are driving your decision in terms of where you live? Many UK graduates move abroad to find the lifestyles and career opportunities they want – and what have they got to lose? The choices shown in Table 5.1 can all impact on your future life and the opportunities within it, so consider which option in each line is most important to you. This is also a good test of how important your career is to you compared with the other elements in life. Would you move tomorrow to where the right career opportunities were for you, regardless of where that was?

Other factors which will impact on your lifestyle are your access to cultural activities, sports and leisure interests, the make up of local people and quality of life in the area. You are unlikely to find somewhere which hits all of these criteria so some degree of compromise will be required. If your career matters to you above all else, you'll move to where the sector is strong and growing fast as opposed to where it is non-existent. If you want to be able to use your language skills in a business and social environment, that will also impact on where you choose to live.

What's the global picture?

Which languages are in demand worldwide? There is increasing demand for Chinese (Mandarin and Cantonese), Japanese, Arabic and Russian. While English is currently the dominant language, Asian and Spanish languages will gain ground in the future. At present,

Table 5.1

Near friends	Same town as friends	Ready to make new friends and keep in touch with old ones
Close to family	Living with parents	Irrelevant – we email and text and they can visit
Cost of living low	Cost of living irrelevant – salary will match	Need to keep this in mind – must find out what living costs are
Opportunity to live cheaply to pay back loans	Have bills, but then doesn't everyone?	Not as important as the job itself
Sector I want to go into is strong in the region with lots of employers	I'll take my chances – I want to stay in the city I did my degree in. I'll take what I find	I'm ready to go to the other side of the world to get the job I want
Staying in home country	Want to go abroad	If the job takes me abroad, so be it
City	Town	Countryside/rural
Irrelevant – the job comes first	Have a strong prefer-ence for where I live	Am absolutely living in this city regardless of opportunities
Short commute to work	Commute is irrelevant – it's the job and em-ployer which matters	Willing to commute within reason
Want to be where I can use my languages in busi-ness and life daily	Want to be able to use my languages at work	Will just be happy us-ing them when I'm on holiday

80 per cent of the Internet is in English but that will drop as other languages gain ground. Don't forget those places where languages are spoken in pockets of countries, such as French in Canada, and Spanish in Latin America apart from Brazil.

The global economy has led employers to outsource huge amounts of work to other parts of the world and form partner-ships, alliances and mergers with others to give them a global stage. A company in China buys one in the UK. You can set up a job in Australia while studying in Paris. Many companies have branches throughout the world, or at least partner organisations they work with, making them even more accessible globally. Across the global organisation, they have standard operating practices and a brand assuring their clients of the same quality service and product wherever they are. At the same time, those same companies need to be in tune with local customs, regulations and understand what works for the locals and what doesn't.

There are 20 *official* languages in the EU alone, among 450 million people. In the EU, the business languages most in demand are German, French, Spanish, Italian and Dutch. The European Commission takes as its watchword, 'The more languages you know, the more of a person you are'. Language skills are important for mobility around the world, effectiveness at work and a country's competitiveness. In November 2005, the European Commission called for action to promote languages and launched a new web portal at http://europa.eu.int/languages/en/home.

There are obvious organisations which recruit translators and interpreters, such as the Court of Justice of the European Communities, the United Nations, the European Commission, the European Parliament, and the European Central Bank. You can find out more information at http://europa.eu.int/languages/en/home, and you may also want to visit http://www.cdt.eu.int, home page for the Translation Centre for the Bodies of the European Union. It has details of job opportunities and details of a traineeship programme for graduates with two or more languages. The European Central Bank will shortly be launching a scheme for post-graduates, preferably with PhDs, in 2006. But there are more small companies springing up in response to the smaller world and the increasing demand for those who can smooth the path of (business) relationship building and success.

Every sector has its hot spots and weak parts so, depending on what you decide to specialise in, you'll need to be prepared to travel to meet your clients. Thus if you intend to go into a specific area, such as the financial services, you may need to relocate to where it is strongest and the opportunities will be greatest: in this case, London, Frankfurt, Paris, Milan, Zurich, Singapore, Hong Kong, New York, Chicago and Boston.

What's the picture in the UK?

The expectation is that there will be significant increases in demand for those at the higher skilled end of the work force, such as managers, professionals, associate professionals and those engaged in technical and service occupations. That said, each region has its growing industries and those in decline. You can find out where your sector's hot spots are by looking at government websites relating to trade and industry, the economy and sites such as the UK Trade and Investment at www.invest.uktradeinvest.gov.uk/.

In areas of traditional and declining industries, redundant skills and depleting resources, governmental Regional Development Agencies (RDAs) are responding by creating initiatives in such areas to regenerate them, boost learning opportunities and facilitate skill acquisition and start-ups. Government bodies such as the RDAs will tell you which sectors are expected to enjoy strong growth or experience a shrinkage – labour market intelligence can be very helpful. Cluster groups and localised graduate websites (see further information) may direct you to useful local networks.

The UK is waking up to the importance of languages. As part of its drive to boost its competitiveness, the UK government has developed a strategy – *Languages for All: Languages for Life* to improve its capability in languages. It has three overall objectives:

1   to improve the teaching and learning of languages;
2   to introduce a new voluntary recognition scheme, the Languages Ladder, to give people credit for their language skills;
3   to increase the number of people studying languages in further and higher education and in work.

The Regional Language Network seeks to promote languages in the workplace, while the Comenius Network supports the National Languages Strategy by mobilising educational partners and stakeholders; broadly speaking, supporting teachers and all those involved in language teaching and learning.

The languages you have will impact on the opportunities open to you. According to CILT, the National Centre for Languages, in the UK, the business languages most in demand are French, German, Italian, Spanish and Dutch. Across the EU, it's German, French and Spanish. In the UK, public service and community organisations have a strong need for the British Sign Language, Hindi, Swahili, Turkish, Urdu and Welsh, in order to serve locals inhabitants. Over 300 languages are now spoken in London, for example, so most organisations, be they private, public or voluntary sector, recognise the need to be able to talk to their customers and clients in their own language.

Be alert to opportunity

Watch the world carefully and keep up-to-date with events and trends. Are there any booming economies which would benefit from your skills and talents? Events which can be disastrous for some people provide opportunities for others. For example, a company makes 500 people redundant, that's unfortunate for the 500 but a great business opportunity for careers coaches and redundancy advisers. Similarly, the Olympics in Beijing in 2008 and London in 2012 will offer great opportunities for people with the right skills.

RDAs are trying to encourage inward investment which should create more employment opportunities. As a literature and language graduate, you could be very helpful to the new business moving to your area which needs people with relevant skills in language and an appreciation of how the UK works. Are there any particular countries they are targeting? Why not make contacts with those who work in the inward investment offices and offer your services?

How are companies using language and literature experts?

Depending on an organisation's requirement, it may call in a language consultant to advise on language training and solutions so that it can solve a problem long term and develop its own in-house expertise. It may also use an agent in another country for the duration of a specific project and then retain links with that agent thereafter. It may employ native speakers and it may take on people who have language skills under their belt.

The evidence is that those of you with languages will be able to command a premium in a couple of aspects when job hunting:

* many firms, when faced with two similar candidates, will claim to take on the one with language skills over the one without;
* many companies now pay extra to those who come with language skills, in some cases £1,000 per annum. Recruitment agencies estimate that some candidates receive between 8 to 20 per cent extra pay for their language skills, depending on the nature of the job and how much they will need to use them in the role.

What initiatives are available to encourage employers to take on graduates?

Governments are investing a lot of money in developing skills and talent, and particularly so at the graduate end of the market. There are many initiatives, programmes, events, websites, help-lines, networking groups, advisory services and more to help you and your peers. In the UK, for example, RDAs are encouraging universities and businesses alike to retain skilled talent in their area and working to raise small companies' awareness of how graduates can benefit them. There is a strong connection between the skill levels in an area and the quality of working opportunities and lifestyle on offer which is why huge efforts are being made to regenerate the weaker areas. Consider initiatives such as the Knowledge Transfer Partnerships (www.ktponline.org.uk) which enable graduates to undertake a project within a company while acquiring management training at the same time, and don't forget internships and work experience programmes (see www.work-experience.com). Many regional graduate careers service providers (see Useful Addresses at the end of this book) offer work placement programmes and schemes designed to boost your employability. This forms part of their drive to encourage graduates to remain in the area after their degree studies. Many private companies are taking up graduates, but what of other enterprises?

What about the not-for-profit organisations?

There are many choices open to you, depending on where and how you want to make an impact and a contribution. The charity sector is booming in the UK. Modern charities need professionals – lawyers, accountants, HR managers, press officers, researchers, IT staff, overseas managers, chief executives – so even if you join the private sector straight after graduating, you can work for a charity later. In fact, this is often your best route in, i.e. to get your professional qualifications and some experience behind you and then go off and change the world. The working conditions experienced by those working for charities has improved considerably in recent years, closing the pay gap with the private sector. Many charities are relocating from the more expensive parts of the UK to other areas. If you want to work for a specific charity, show willing and do voluntary work first, to prove your worth and your commitment. Find out who the decision makers are so that you can network with the right people. The sector is for you if job satisfaction and contribution is more important than money.

Many graduates are working in the fair trade revolution, or setting up social enterprises to boost causes they feel strongly about. The latter are not-for-profit organisations, but they really can make a difference. You could also contribute to another country's development, working with the people who live there. Examples of work volunteers may do include teaching, care and community, medicine, business, journalism, law and sport.

Working for the community

From housing associations to local government, there are opportunities with graduate training schemes, management training schemes and other ways 'in' without the graduate tag. In the UK, the Government has increased the number of jobs in the sector by nearly 600,000 since coming to power in 1997, most significantly in those areas where it has a strong foothold in power. Opportunities range from working in the police force, health service, education, management, trade and enterprise.

Look around you and consider the languages people speak in the area you wish to work in. Many communities in the UK, for example, need translators and interpreters in languages such as Turkish, Polish, Kurdish Sorani and Albanian. But thanks to the Internet, there is a need for rarer languages to be translated too. The Chartered Institute of Linguists Educational Trust has a list of languages it will assess for the Diploma in Public Service Interpreting and you'll find more information on its website.

Analyse the sector you wish to join and consider the size of the average company in it

The size of the niche area or sector will make a difference as to how competitive it is to get into. You may need to move abroad to get entry into your desired career or into an allied industry in your home country if that's where you want to stay. The size of the niche area or sector will make a difference as to how competitive it is to get into. There may be 30,000 PR companies in the UK, for example, but 300,000 banks, so you could deduce that it will be more difficult to get into a PR company than a bank, particularly as many employers take graduates of any discipline.

Finding suitable employment opportunities

Employers use a range of methods to recruit employees and you should use a range of methods in your job hunting. Companies may create links with schools, colleges and universities through careers fairs and presentations, take on staff via their own websites or those of agencies, advertisements in the local press, looking at on-spec applications, finding students through work experience, internships and secondments. They could spread the net wider, hooking potential recruits in through agencies, the national press and specialist trade journals; some are even using Radio and TV adverts.

Having identified where you want to work, search out those employers!

If you use a multitude of methods to find employers and seek the role you crave, you're more likely to land it. Stick to one or two, and it will take longer to do so. Walk into every circle shown in Figure 5.1 to hunt for the opportunities you're looking for and persist in your efforts until you find success.

In addition, you should:

1   run a search for all the relevant employers using all the means at your disposal, including Kompass and Dun and Bradstreet, both excellent online resources of business and company information;
2   use your local library which should have sector reports, books and information about the local area, trade and national magazines, phone and trade directories;
3   register for any email alerts with online agencies to pick up new jobs which come in that might interest you.

Hint: You can do a search for businesses at http://local.google. com/. Use several search terms to maximise the effectiveness of your search.

Figure 5.1

Go on the alert for vacancies

Of course you can register your details with various online agencies, associations and groups, which have the facility to enable employers to search out someone with the skills and talents they need. This enables you to receive email alerts when new jobs come in and to browse the vacancies available and make contact with the appropriate agency or employer. Online and printed directories can help you identify small and medium-sized companies to consider. You can often register with sites for a fee and acquire access to hundreds of jobs with daily alerts and lots of great links and careers information. An example is www.broadcastfreelancer.com. Keep your personal details up-to-date, so that they reflect any extra experience and skills you're acquiring. In addition, many websites have details of opportunities.

Going through recruitment companies

Recruitment agencies are selected by employers to find recruits for them. Many employers have long-standing relationships with agencies, so agency consultants build up an extensive knowledge of what the employer is like to work for and what sort of career path candidates can expect upon successful application and starting.

Agencies offer various services to their candidates, including help with CVs (although some agencies have their own particular CV format to send to clients) and profiling so that you can work out what sort of work would suit you best. Your consultant should have a clear idea of trends in the sector and how your career will fit into it. He or she should enjoy strong links with the industry. Many offer training, and some run networking evenings. It's essential to remember that your consultant is human, too, so treat him or her as you would like to be treated.

Online recruitment has become big business. Many online agencies and professional bodies offer the facility of receiving email alerts, enabling you to receive notice that new (relevant) vacancies are available. Newspapers and trade magazines also have online vacancy boards and often send newsletters. You may also be able to post your CV on some sites for potential employers to view.

If you want to get into a specific industry, look for agencies which are active in and focus on it, with a good track record – they are more likely to have a strong network and an ear to the ground for opportunities.

You can quickly access a huge number of agencies in specific sectors by visiting http://www.agencycentral.co.uk which has agencies listed under sector and also has a full list of agencies offering graduate positions.

Go to where the action is, ready to sell your talents

This includes careers events and trade fairs, not just those surrounding the area of employment and shows anywhere you are likely to find companies involved in the business. Many of these have seminars on starting your own business and marketing your own work, selling yourself and building good client relationships. Many events will provide a forum for you to get out there, meet and greet and hand people your business card. You can find a list of the larger shows at www.biztradeshows.com and find details by industry or country. There's also www.eventseye.com, another global listing of events by location, topic or date. Check too your local business network sites because they also may list sector specific events and exhibitions. In the UK, www.exhibitions.co.uk has details of fairs and exhibitions. If you're planning to go as an exhibitor, www.businesslink.gov.uk has some first-class tips on how to make the most of a show. For details of events in the film and television industry, visit www.creative.fastchannel.com.

Plan for a successful event

When you approach stand-holders, an introductory chat about their company and what it's developing and working on can quickly lead to a sentence or two about yourself and your career goals. Regardless of whether you're going to a trade show or careers event, tips for a successful show include:

- Pre-register online to avoid lengthy queues.
- Identify the people you want to meet and visit their websites *before* you go. On arrival, visit their stands *first* while you're fresh and full of energy.
- Create a business card to hand out. Put your contact details (email and mobile number) and your most recent or relevant educational qualification on one side with niche areas; and the sort of company you're looking to work for, plus skills you have to contribute on the other.
- Prepare questions to ask before you go to avoid mumbling and stumbling over awkward introductory waffle. *'What advice do you have for someone in my position?'* and *'What job hunting strategies can you suggest I use?'* can be two helpful questions to get insider information and give you other routes to follow.
- Ask open questions. *'Do you recruit graduates of any discipline?'* is a closed question requiring a simple yes or no answer; you won't learn much. *'What degrees do you particularly look to recruit?'* is hard to answer with a yes or no. As an open question, it gives you more information and enables you to engage the person you're talking to in further conversation.

- Don't start off by asking *'What can your company do for me?'* or *'What can your company offer me?'*. Promote yourself as someone who has a lot to contribute to the right employer.
- If someone looks busy, wait until they are quieter.
- Talk to people in the café areas. Make some small talk about the fair – *'What a great opportunity to meet people!' 'What a great venue!' 'Isn't it good to sit down?' 'Are you here as an exhibitor?' 'What does your company do?' 'I'll stop by and see you at your stand!' 'Could I contact you next week and ask for some of your time?'* Smaller companies may not have a stand, but you might bump into a representative from one if you start talking to people in the café areas.
- If you get stuck talking to people who are being negative about your general situation, *'There are too many of us graduating!'* politely say goodbye and wish them luck and walk away. Focus on what you *do* want and ways to increase your chances of succeeding in getting it. Sitting and moping isn't one of them.
- When the event is over, walk away and reflect over what you've learnt about the opportunities available and yourself. Bring together action points and carry them through. Business cards create dust if unused; you want them to create results.
- Write and thank the people you met at the show by email or letter. If you have a web CV, you can attach the address under your contact details at the bottom. After the event, identify those people you need to follow up and contact them.

Heading to other shores – working abroad

This may be particularly appropriate if you're thinking, *'Well, my industry is dead in this country. So what now?'* In this case, you have a number of choices before you. You can switch to an allied industry, in which your degree may still come in useful, or you can change altogether, or start your own business. Could you, for example, export anything which is needed by the industry in those regions where it is flourishing?

Ten questions to ask include:

1   What is the local job market like?
2   How do employers recruit staff there? What is involved in the recruitment process?

3   How should I write a CV for that country? What should I include?

4   What organisations and websites can I turn to for advice and information (e.g. Prospects and Hobsons)?

5   Does my professional body or trade organisation have any relevant links in the country I wish to work in? What support can it give me?

6   How will my current qualifications transfer? Will they be accepted? Many professional bodies are working with other countries across borders to ensure the smooth transfer and recognition of qualifications from one nation to another. Are these countries more interested in experience?

7   How does the working environment differ? What is acceptable behaviour and what is not?

8   What level of job would I have with the competences I have got?

9   Will I need to take additional tests to prove my competence in my new country before I can start work?

10   Where in the world will my knowledge and skills be needed in the future?

Put *willing to re-locate* on your CV or business card but be prepared to actually do it. If you're focusing in on one country and you satisfy visa requirements, say so on your CV or covering letter (see www.workpermit.com). Look out for events and newspaper supplements promoting life or companies abroad. Use your network to help you get work overseas, read journals and newspapers and make use of embassies and state employment services such as http://europa.eu.int/eures. The European Job Mobility Portal is one of the places where European candidates can see an employer's vacancy and employers can multi-search for CVs which may meet their needs. It links the public employment services in Europe and helps people take up work in other member states of the EEA. It has lots of information on jobs, learning, labour markets, health, registering for work when you arrive and working conditions.

You could also sign up with a recruitment agency that has international offices or connections, or go through an organisation offering placements abroad, such as GAP, or simply do it yourself. Don't forget to tap into any twinning arrangements and Chamber of Commerce organisations (www.chamberonline.co.uk/). These have links to trade organisations and research they've undertaken into markets abroad. Their site has details of all the UK Chambers, overseas Chambers in the UK, British Chambers of Commerce overseas and the Council of British Chambers of Commerce in Continental Europe. It also has an excellent export zone and business services on offer.

Returning home later on

The various locations you choose to work need to be kept in mind when you're considering where to settle later in life. Sooner or later, you may want to return home. Watch for any trends or new laws or regulations there which may impede on your ability to return when the time comes. Consider the financial implications for your future. How will working abroad affect any pension due to you later in life, be it state or private? Read *Working Abroad: The Complete Guide to Overseas Employment* by Jonathan Reuvid (see Further Reading at the end of this book).

Your next steps

1   List employers in the sector you wish to work in and research in the country you want to work in.
2   Develop a short list by researching them through the Internet, careers fairs, finding out about their products and services through your network and news items.
3   Who do you know, or which sector networks could you tap into, to acquire an introduction to these companies?

Moving things forward ... do you, don't you?

Find out more about the organisation and its career opportunities, but don't confine your research to the company's website. Delve further and wider for any mention of it in the local, national or international media. Most employers try to provide as much information as they can about their organisation to job hunters so that the latter can ensure they are applying to the right sort of company for them. Why not see if you can get in touch with someone appropriate at the company to see if you can visit and look around, and talk about the opportunities available?

Questions to ask of a potential employer

1   What is its mission and what does it want to do and achieve? Does it excite you?

2   What messages does it give you about its values and what it deems to be important? What values does the organisation or company portray in its advertising, literature, image and brand? Look for evidence that it upholds these values. Do they excite you?

3   What is the size of the organisation and how will that impact on the way people work and the opportunities within it?

4   Where is it located? Is it spread over a number of sites?

5   What is the structure and hierarchy; is there just the one company or are there a number of subsidiary companies within one group?

6   How is it organised? A small company may have one person looking after IT, marketing, sales, web design and HR which would put a generalist business degree to excellent use; a large one will have a department of people for each of these elements enabling you to focus on one area.

7   What is the company's financial position? If it is not healthy, your career there may be short. What are its strengths, weaknesses, opportunities and threats?

8   What sort of people work for it? Look at employee profiles. What do they get involved with outside of work? How do they describe themselves, the company and their roles?

Find out what the company is doing to be innovative and competitive. Where does it see itself going and what is its place in the market? If there is no evidence of such activities, ask yourself whether the company will exist in five years' time? Careful research into its finances and diplomatic questioning at interview time can help you assess such a state.

Eight key questions to ask yourself

1   What could you contribute to this organisation in terms of skills and qualities?

2   Is this the sort of place you'd look forward to walking into every Monday morning?

3   Could you see yourself working for them in five years' time?

4   Can they offer you the future you're looking for?
5   What would you need to do to make the career progress you want to enjoy? What support would you get from the company?
6   How could you secure a foot in the door?
7   Is there a vacancy right now you could apply for or will you need to make contact on spec?
8   What actions are you going to take next and when?

You could multiply the opportunities before you if you consider working for an organisation short term, perhaps on a contract basis or freelance basis to get your foot in the door. Part-time work will leave you free to job hunt for the role you really want, or to develop your own business while bringing some money in. A small company may not have enough work to warrant taking someone on full time but it may offer you freelance work. Think laterally and creatively when you're job hunting.

Starting your own business

There is more help around than ever before for those with an entrepreneurial spirit but still too many start-ups fail for lack of sufficient advice and research. The BusinessLink network in England helps small companies and start-ups. Visit www.businesslink.gov.uk to find your local link. There's information on setting up a business, writing a business plan, accessing funding, growing your business and even selling it on. There are also links to the sister organisations in Scotland, Wales and Northern Ireland.

Consider initiatives

Aside from Flying Start (see page 43), other national examples of organisations helping people to set up on their own include Shell LiveWIRE, the Prince's Trust, Start-ups and the Prime Initiative for the over 50s (see Useful Addresses at the end of this book). Some initiatives may be national in nature, others very local.

Eight questions to consider

1   What's your vision and what do you want to achieve with this business?
2   What are your products and services?
3   What do you need to get up and running, e.g.:
    *   somewhere to work from;
    *   equipment needed to set up (you may have a lot of this already);
    *   computer/lap top/ipod;
    *   communications – Internet, phone, fax;
    *   marketing and publicity materials – possibly a website, business cards, brochures, membership of professional and business networks;
    *   insurance, professional indemnity and public liability;
    *   training;
    *   a salary/wage?
4   Who can support you?
5   What new skills and knowledge will you need?
6   Who are your competitors?
7   What research do you need to do?
8   Where will you get funding from?

Summary action points

Move your thinking further forward:

1   What are agencies in the region doing to encourage businesses to take on graduates, particularly those in my sector?
2   How much do I know about the work I want to do and how to get 'in' to it?
3   Where are most of the employers located in this sector?
4   Which other areas are showing a rapid growth?
5   What am I doing to enjoy life and have time out while I'm working towards my goals?

Chapter 6

Proving yourself

From scholar to worker

One minute you're a student and the next you're not. You may choose to have some time out or get going on with your career straightaway, but whichever path you take, there's a big difference between the two. The earlier you start preparing for life after your university days, the easier it will be to settle in work and life afterwards.

Making the psychological switch

It's time to leave some habits behind and start behaving differently. You've probably had a fantastic time, and learnt a great deal, but if you were a full-time student, it's time to take stock and recognise that the fun days – and yes, we know you worked hard – are behind you and its time to move on. You may be feeling a keen sense of loss, a wonderment of what comes next, a sure certainty that the world's your oyster and there's lots of opportunity out there, but how on earth will any of it relate to you back in your parents' home?

There is quite a switch from being a student to becoming an employee or self-employed, because the impact of your work and how well you do it affects other people, as shown in Table 6.1.

The 'learning to do' referred to above relates to those things you cannot be taught until you start work, such as product knowledge specific to the organisation you join. But at the very least, employers want to know that you know how to behave at work and that you understand what work is like.

At work, you'll still get the person who does it all at the last minute, those who are indecisive, bullies, patronising or negative, who spout *'We've always done it like this',* and see no reason to change. There are the moody, sulky and lazy, working alongside power-crazy, highly competitive workaholics and you'll need to deal

Table 6.1

As a student		As an employee
Studying	and	Working
Being a student	and	an employee/employer
Learning	and	Doing or learning to do ...
Student responsibilities	and	Responsibilities at work towards: team; clients, customers; company/employer; your own colleagues, peers
The hours you choose to work	and	The hours you're expected to work
Holidays	and	Average 4 weeks holiday – in the US, probably 1 or 2 weeks in the first few years
The way you dress and behave	and	The image and behaviour that's right and appropriate for work
Long-term personal goals	and	Vision, mission, targets need the goodwill and motivation of everyone on board
Rules and regulations in your university	and	Employment laws, health and safety, professional regulations
Meeting deadlines – it's just you that suffers	and	Meeting deadlines – other people are depending on you
The pace of life – you can dictate it	and	The pace of work is dictated by the industry and demands of clients and customers. Your day can change dramatically on receipt of a phone call. People expect fast responses. Are you adaptable and flexible?
Your performance – it affects just you	and	Your performance can affect that of your team and the company – it can clinch a deal, save the company money
You can control pretty much most things in your life	and	There are many things you can control but equally there are many you cannot

with them all. Your skills and talents in motivating and managing people will be well tested as you progress, and work to bring out the best in your team. You'll need your influencing and persuading skills to encourage those around you to see the benefits of what you want to do. But your experiences at university will have given you a good start in speaking up for yourself and getting along with people from all different backgrounds and with their own aspirations. Add work experience in a real live work situation, and you can put the above skills into place and make the psychological switch.

Transferable skills are essential to enjoy life and excel at work

List everything you've done during your university days and you will be astonished at what you've achieved formally and informally. To do it all, you will have used skills which transfer from one aspect of life to another, such as communication. To communicate effectively with clients and colleagues, family and friends, you need to express yourself clearly, orally and in writing through email, letter and fax. You need to be able to empathise with and understand the needs of others.

Rank the transferable skills in Figure 6.1 in order of your strength, 5 being the strongest.

Now find evidence for each one looking through your list of extra-curricular activities, voluntary efforts, work experience and academic work. Which are your strengths? Which are your weaknesses and how are you tackling those? Take each transferable skill and give an example of a time when you've used it. Consider all the angles you might be asked about it.

Have you made the most of university life?

University days offer the chance to create a life out of a blank canvas. Employers will be looking to see how you occupied your time and what you learnt from your activities. They'll be looking for evidence of your passion for your subject, such as which shows you've been to, competitions you've entered, any writing you've done in your spare time (if appropriate) and what projects you have done over and above your coursework which might be of interest to potential employers or clients and customers. What were the modes of learning you used which could transfer over to the workplace,

	5	4	3	2	I
Organising/planning					
Communicating, orally					
Communicating, written					
Learning					
Creativity					
Decision making					
Self-motivation					
Strategic planning					
Handling change					
Problem solving					
Team working					
Leadership					
Adaptability, flexibility					
Self-awareness					
Commercial awareness					

Figure 6.1

such as giving presentations, undertaking research, debating a point in seminars and tutorials, critiquing your work, taking an idea from conception to fruition, working in a team to solve a problem?

Effectiveness and high performance at work is built on the right attitude, a professional competence and approach, product and sector knowledge, a *drive* to make things happen and soft skills. At university, you develop skills through various academic and extra-curricular activities. To progress your career, you need continued exposure to different experiences and the right training and personal development, all of which continue to expand your capabilities, push back your comfort zones and build on your soft or transferable skills. Self-awareness, self-promotion and self-presentation also count, along with keeping abreast of career developments and news in your field. Figure 6.2 shows how university and work link together incorporating all these elements.

Throughout your life, both in and out of work, you'll need to manage a number of ingredients, as shown in Table 6.2.

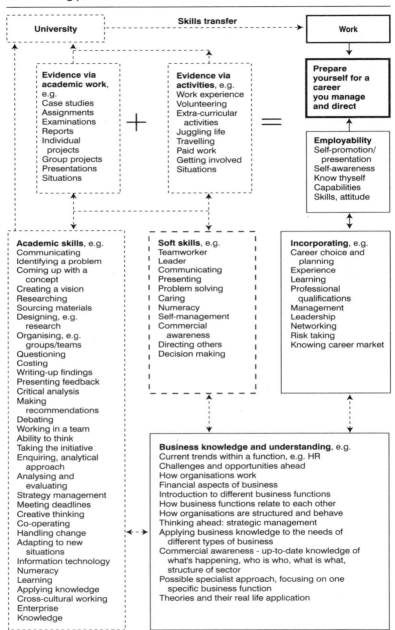

Figure 6.2

Table 6.2

Yourself	Information technology
People	Resources
Teams	Materials
Time	Projects
Money	Deadlines
Your energy	Research
The client's expectations	The facilities around you
Your future	Your suppliers

Who are you?

This is not just about your qualifications and experience to date. They certainly contribute and play a part, but this is more about how you arrived at the whole-rounded individual you are now. It's not about *'Well, I completed my UCAS form and made my six choices, and then sat and prayed that I'd get in to my first choice!'* It's about, how did you come to apply at all? What and who moulded your decisions and what did you need *within yourself* to get to where you are today? What resources did you pull out of your body, heart, mind and soul to make your degree happen and how can you build on them and use them to maximum effect throughout your life? Who did you work alongside as you strove to achieve your mutual goals? *(That's teamwork!)*

It's also about your values, and what matters to you. After all, you must have chosen the path you took for a reason. So what lies behind and within you, what makes you tick, what drives, inspires and motivates you? What challenges and dramas have you faced? How have you tackled them? *(That's problem solving.)* If you wrote your life story, what particular achievements would you want your readers to know about? What journeys would you want to tell them about? How can you show them that you've turned your plans into action? Have you done a stint of travelling, or juggled study and work at the same time? *(Shows adaptability and flexibility, planning and organisation.)* When have you really had to knuckle down and make things happen? Were there times when you kept going when everything else seems to be going against you? How many times have you failed at something – anything – and you've tried and tried again until success came your way? *(Persistence, motivation, drive, resilience.)* What changes have you dealt with in your life; if you've driven them yourself how have you tapped into your drive and energy and passion to make them happen? If they happened outside your control, how did you handle them? *(Resilience, ability to cope with change).* What negative experiences have you been through that you've learnt from? How could you show a stranger the person you truly are, as opposed to a bunch of qualifications listed neatly on a page? *(That's written communication, persuading, influencing, expressing.)* What sort of person would they see? It's these qualities that you need to bring out in your CV or interviews when applying for jobs or courses. *(That's self-promotion.)*

It's also about those things which prompted you to make the choices you have in work, play and leisure, and in the friends you hang around with. *(That shows what motivates you.)* What circumstances have you grown up in which have influenced you, your actions, your choices and the messages you've taken on board about yourself, life and the opportunities ahead? *(Decision making and action planning skills here.)* What have you done to challenge them? *(You don't settle for just anything!)* What have you done to help yourself? These sorts of things have all contributed to make up the person you are by influencing and moulding you over the years. It will also show you that being successful – however you define success – takes tremendous hard graft, self-discipline and continual, sustained effort. Without ingredients such as these, success all too often feels hollow, empty and unsatisfying. Look at all the times you've been proactive and what the results were. Look at the opportunities you created for yourself by getting off your backside and making something happen. *(Taking the initiative.)* If you want to be successful in the way you envisage success, you need to do that again and again.

However, you've studied towards your degree, be it full time, part time or by distance learning, so congratulate yourself. Go out with a group of friends and sink a few drinks. But take time to quietly, independently and proudly assess what you've achieved and, crucially, the characteristics in your personality, the motivators and drivers which have empowered you to success, such as persistence, determination and curiosity. You've had the endurance to get. through a degree, and developed the ability to network, form working relationships fast, to take responsibility for your own career development and learning and to be resourceful.

Acknowledge your strengths and resources in writing

Written down, they will give you a lift, especially if you're feeling low. Whatever stage of life you're at, you'll need to draw on all your resources to create the future you want. Get ready to dig deep and raise your energy levels, standards, focus, persistence and drive to a higher level to propel yourself into making it happen. Finally, you'll be able to tell employers more succinctly what lies behind the person you are – and the person you want to be, thereby selling yourself more effectively. Self-presentation and promotion is an important skill at work today.

The power of work experience

Work experience strengthens your hand in the employment market, particularly if it is targeted towards the career you intend to follow and structured in such a way that you can learn and put the theory you have learnt on your degree course into practice. Employers can see you in action for themselves: the way you walk and talk, think and act, behave and motivate, initiate and inspire, work and apply your new-found knowledge. They want to see how effective you are and how you achieve results. In fact, employers rate work experience and internships as a highly effective way to find graduate recruits. There are many schemes on offer throughout the year for varying periods of time. Their entry is often highly competitive, requiring the same professional approach and strategy to achieve success as job hunting.

The small and medium enterprise (SME) market in its own right can give you the chance to put your foot in the door. There may be a scheme running in your area to help companies and graduates benefit each other. The National Council for Work Experience has a lot more information on its website (www.work-experience.org). Also look for opportunities to gain experience through professional bodies and trade associations' websites. Check out www.step.org. uk which arranges placements with companies for a year or shorter periods of time. Many of the websites listed in this book have details of work placements, internships and residencies and you need to get to know which sites are most suitable for you. Internships, residencies and work experience placements are very competitive and it can be hard to survive for three months with just your travel expenses.

However, it is an excellent way in, so consider it as an investment, just as your university studies are.

You don't have to sign up for a specific scheme. You could approach a company directly for experience, which may be a great way to get into a smaller company that may not be aware of opportunities to join placement schemes. Keep trying and persisting.

1   Identify what it is that you need to practise at work – are there particular skills you want to use?
2   Pinpoint what you will bring to the employer – enthusiasm and a passion for what you're doing are a start.
3   Give the employer examples of what you can do and what you would like to do, so that he has a menu of choices.
4   Show him what you have done so far, so that he has a clear idea of what you're capable of.
5   Give an allotted time-scale but be flexible.
6   Find out if the company has a project which needs to be done which no-one else has time to do.
7   Ask for an assessment of your work at the end, so that the employer can write a testimonial and you can together work out what you have achieved and got out of the placement.

Work experience should play a central role in your sales strategy when you start job hunting. It shows that you know what you're letting yourself in for. You can talk about your experiences and achievements at interview and demonstrate your effectiveness through the job-specific and transferable skills you've used. You can prove how you can be relied on to get results, to make things happen and to achieve. You can prove your passion for, and belief in, what you're doing and that you've got your hands dirty. Talk the lingo, understand the frustrations, challenges, issues, opportunities and threats. As a rule, the longer and more relevant the experience, the more beneficial it will be.

If you've found a work experience on your own, turn it into a constructive learning time. Identify what you want out of it and what you have to offer before you approach an employer. Find out if there is a project you can do to practise specific skills and put your course theory into practice. Observe closely and ask the right questions, and you'll acquire an insight into how the different parts of the organisation pull together as everyone works to fulfil the mission or vision set out in its profile.

You can pick up the language relevant to the sector and the organisation or company itself. You can pick up business lingo relevant to the business world with terms such as 'profit and loss', 'added value', 'key performance indicators', and you'll understand what they are. Listening skills are important if you're to pick up the language and way of working specific to the business. Each one has its own terminology relating to its systems, protocol, meetings, hierarchy, and many have their own intranet. Work experience gives you an insight into how companies function and helps you make those all-important contacts. *'I've got a friend who works in PR. Shall I mention you to her? She could give you a call for a chat.'*

Finally, remember that working at the bottom of the organisation is a great way to learn how the various parts work, who the key decision makers are and why the bottom line is so important.

Work to close any skills gaps

Every industry has its problems recruiting staff with the right skills. In many niche areas, there are cluster groups, forums and groups of employers, industry specialists and training providers who are trying to tackle the problem and encourage employers to offer (graduates) a way in and a structured learning environment. Ideas which are being developed include apprenticeship programmes, business realisation schemes, training programmes and career-entry initiatives. Go to the heart of the industry to find out what is being undertaken in yours. Skillset (www.skillset.org) for the audio visual industries has great examples of such initiatives.

Meantime, why not show someone who works in the sector a copy of your CV and ask them where your skills gaps are? How can you go about closing them? It may be that a short training programme will do the trick, or perhaps a stint of work experience with exposure to a particular area will help.

What behaviours and practices do you need to elicit to make your 'it' happen?

* Be very determined. Push for your corner, but remain polite.
* Get focused.
* Be prepared to sacrifice something else in your life so that you can give what you really want the hours it deserves. True

friends will understand if you can only meet them once a fortnight or once a week.

Go out there and start building up your experience in any skills you wish to use at work or in your own business

1   Start acquiring clients and earning money for the skills you have. Ask them for feedback on how you handled them and their business, from acquiring a commission, to discussing pricing, invoicing, and their pleasure and satisfaction with the end product. Get practice in promoting and selling your skills.

2   While you're looking for clients or hunting for a permanent position, build up evidence of commissions by doing things for yourself, for example working on projects in the area you want to get into.

3   Get your work out there where it can be seen by entering competitions and offering to do any relevant work for charities. Hundreds of small local charities struggle on without the support and back-up of a large organisation. Find out if a local charity has a project it needs doing but doesn't have the resources to do it and needs your skills and talents.

4   Offer to do some work for a heavily discounted rate in return for a testimonial to put on your marketing literature or website.

If you want to set up a business while working, do it while others sleep

Consider the number of wannabe writers who rise at 4.30 a.m. to write in the hope they can chuck in the day job once they hook a deal with a publisher or get that e-book up on the web. If something is important enough to you, you'll *make* time for it, schedule it in and, inevitably, sacrifice something along the way to achieve your goals and ambitions. Keep the dream alive and work to turn it into reality. Nobody said it was easy.

Start behaving and immersing yourself in the field you want to be in

If you're job hunting, devote full-time effort to the task. Keep your ambitions and goals at the forefront of your mind, or they will lose their prominence in your heart and it will take more effort to make them happen, especially if you consider yourself to be in a 'lower level' role right now. Position yourself to get out of it, either by moving or staying put, or one of two things can happen (see Figure 6.3).

Network, network, network

Take the wheel of networking in Figure 6.4. At some time in your life, you may focus on one segment more than others; you may want to add or delete a segment. Aim for a balanced wheel, so that you can tap into the support you need for a healthy, balanced life and successful, happy career. Tap into every corner to see if any (albeit unexpectedly) can provide you with the opportunity you need to truly kick off your career and life in the direction you want it to go.

1   What are you doing to make something happen in each segment to create the career and life you want?
2   Which do you need to focus on *more* to get the results you need and make the connections you want?

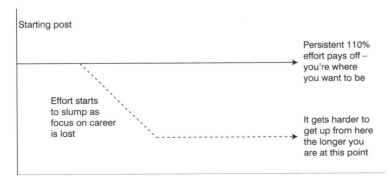

Figure 6.3

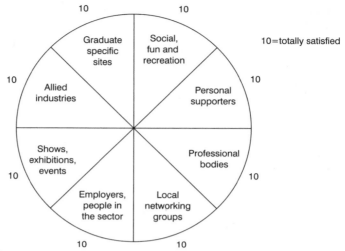

Figure 6.4

3   Which section(s) should the *hub* of your network be at right now so that you can tackle the most important and urgent issues in your life?

4   How much activity do you have in it or them at the moment? How much time are you spending on accessing them and getting yourself known? How often are you making new contacts in it? Which is yielding the best results?

5   What do you need to do to make sure the sector you need to have the strongest network in is up to par to get the results you need in your life?

Prepare your experience to date

Make sure you have some features to show potential editors and employers. Are you ready to talk about work you've done which will be relevant to potential employers, such as editing a club's magazine, writing for the local paper, doing work experience for hospital radio, taking a short course in marketing your own business? Can you show how you're always working at your craft and what you've done to make inroads into the sector? View your experience as a marketing tool, a showpiece, and be proud of it.

Showing off your work

Create a CD which is easy to navigate and which holds details of your work on it, together with a brief description surrounding each piece. Include your contact details and a CV. Keep adding to it, so that you have regular new pieces of work to show off and discuss.

Temping your way to a career

Like work experience, temping gives you the opportunity to show what you can do and will often lead to a permanent role.

Five steps to getting 'in' to a company through temping

1   Hook up with a specialist agency which focuses on the specific sector you want to work in. If you're still thinking about what you want to do, sign up with a high street name which covers many sectors to broaden your insight and experience. A visit to the company's website will help you assess its strengths and focus and track record.

2   When you sign up with an agency, dress as if you're going for an interview so that the agency knows it can send you out with confidence. Your consultant should talk through your skills, competencies and career goals. Ask how often and by what method you should keep in touch. Check emails and your mobile regularly for messages. Try to get two or three-week or month assignments together in one sector to enhance your CV's consistency. Be more flexible at first and show you can be trusted first before you get choosey.

3   Look for ways to put the knowledge and skills you've acquired through your university experience into practice in the company you're with. Ask the company for projects or you can do them voluntarily to help develop your skills. Reflect weekly on skills and knowledge you're acquiring. Which environments have you thrived most in? What have you achieved? Get feedback from your agency and the company you're with.

4   Update your CV regularly and ensure the agency has a copy so that they can send out your most recent one. Focus on your transferable skills and consider exactly how they will help the sector you want to join.

5   Consider what you need to start doing to make the overall experience more effective and to take you closer to achieving your goals. What strategies can you employ to make these happen?

Many people find work exhausting enough without doing career planning back home too. But this is where 110 per cent commitment and effort will get you to where you want to be, while the 90 per cent won't, so raise your standard.

How do you take time out to go for interviews?

Companies are paying for you to be there and do the job they need you to do, not to keep disappearing for interviews with others – who may be their competitors. If you keep calling in sick, this makes you look unreliable in the eyes of the agency *and* employer. Many companies will interview people first thing in the morning or late afternoon. Work extra hours the day before or after at your temporary assignment. Give your temporary employer as much notice as possible. Work at 110 per cent and they won't want to lose you. Ask your agency for advice as to how to best handle the situation.

Don't wait for doors to open for you. Get out there and start knocking on doors to connect to the opportunities you want while you're working or studying.

Learn from others you deem to be successful – how do they do it?

Seek out those who are where you wish to be. They've done it. But *how did they get there?* People love to talk about themselves and many will see it as a compliment if you ask their advice. If they see passion and enthusiasm in you, they'll be more than happy to help.

Go to careers shows, relevant trade shows and exhibitions and talk to people. Be friendly and interested. How did they get to where they are today? What advice would they have for you? What has their career path been and what are the three most important factors which have contributed to their success? Contact people you deem successful. What lessons have they learnt along the way that they can pass on to you? Follow up major show winners with an email to congratulate them and then ask their advice. Read Sarah Brown's book, *Moving on up*, with advice and stories from leaders in many sectors on how they got to the top and what it takes.

Get ahead – get a mentor

Mentors have been there, done it and got the t-shirt. They can be an invaluable source of help, advice and contacts and many mentors get a great deal from the process themselves. A mentor will talk to you about your goals, aspirations and how you can get there. They will help you stay on track and keep focused. There are lots of mentor programmes available through many specialist networking groups and you should look at various websites listed throughout this book to find one which suits your needs. Mentoring can be done face-to-face or over the telephone. If you want to get ahead, learn from those who will make you think about what you're doing, asking you questions which you wouldn't think of asking yourself.

Heading for self-employment?

Consider these questions:

- Name three companies which are success stories (they can be any size)?
- What makes them successful?
- What works well for them? What doesn't?
- What makes customers and clients turn to them for products and services?
- What can you learn from them and apply to your own business?

Now let's do this exercise differently:

- Name three companies which have not been successful or which are going through a really rough time?
- Where are they going wrong?
- What are they trying to do to put things right?
- What has put customers and clients off them for products and services?
- What can you learn from them and apply to your own business?

Brainstorm with friends or join forces with other graduates to see what you can learn from them and their outlook.

Have a go!

Opportunities to get a lucky break don't happen unless you work to create them. For example, BBC Talent run an annual competition for people trying to get into film and TV. If you don't enter, you're clearly not going to win. It's a competitive world out there, so start competing. There are a large number of sites with advice and opportunities for writers, including the BBC's Writers Room at www.bbc.co.uk/writersroom/ and Lighthouse at www.lighthouse.org.uk. *The Writers and Artists Yearbook* has the names of many companies in radio, television, theatre and publishing, plus awards, competitions and more – you should find a copy in your local reference library.

Summary action points

Turn your experience from an academic one into a work-related one which means something to employers and gets you in the right mind-set.

1   Look to see how you can start living the working day so far as possible.
2   Identify steps you can take which will bring you closer to the role you want.
3   Review your progress to date in areas such as: your own self-awareness and how far that has come; your picture of your career and life in the next three to five years; how your network has changed; and how far you've researched potential employers (or courses) to apply to.
4   How can you change your behaviour to get the success you want? What could you do differently?

Chapter 7

Promoting yourself

The next stage, as you prepare to sell yourself, is to consider questions such as:

- What can you do to boost your chances of success?
- What can you control? What is outside your control? (For example, you can control the time you spend job hunting and where you choose to job hunt.)

If you respond to an advert in a newspaper, you *can* control the quality of your application, but you *cannot* control the numbers of applicants applying for the same post. You can choose to demonstrate your ability to communicate clearly and present your case well by submitting a well thought out, easily read and well expressed application.

Turn your skills and talents into a marketable commodity and promote the skills you need to get the work

A degree in languages and literature opens the door to many careers, but you need to remember that you should promote the skills most of all which will be core to the work you'll be doing. If you're applying for a role in which your language skills will simply complement your work, the employer will want to know about the other skills you have and consider your language competences to be a bonus.

If, however, your language abilities are core and essential to the job in hand, then you *will* need put more emphasis on your language abilities, but you'll need to emphasise skills such as working to deadlines, time management, accuracy, proof reading, cultural awareness and sector knowledge. As an example, if you want to translate legal documents, you'll need to show that you speak the language of the legal world and *understand it*.

Think about the role you want and its core activities, and make the bulk of your CV and application relevant to that, while outlining any additional useful points which may hook an employer's interest, such as your language skills. If you are a post-graduate, you will need to be particularly adept at selling the skills and qualities you have acquired as a result of your extra qualification, such as self-direction, resilience and initiative.

Bear in mind that if you claim to have language skills, or apply for any sort of a role in which language skills are required, then you will almost inevitably be tested in them at some stage or other.

If you're applying for work abroad, find out how employers recruit in that country and what they look for in an application. Some won't be at all interested in your hobbies and interests, while others will. Show you've thought about the way they operate and recruit. The extra effort you put in will pay dividends.

Remember, enlist several ways of job hunting – don't put all your eggs into one basket. Aim to do something with each method at least once a week.

Once you've identified a vacancy or course you would like to take or an employer you would like to work for:

1   Identify any deadlines so that you can work out what to do when, and pinpoint what needs to be done;

2   Assess the skills, knowledge, acumen and attitude your potential employer needs by researching their organisation carefully;

3   Identify the evidence you need to paint the picture of your capabilities and aspirations from your research, life resources, characteristics to date, work experience, voluntary work, travel, leisure, team efforts and projects;

4   If you need to include a CV with your application, write it out until you are comfortable with it; produce a one-page letter of application and anything else required. In your one-page letter, highlight the skills and experience you have which are relevant to the role you're applying for, and explain why the company you're writing to appeals to you. Mention something about the company which shows you know a bit about them – perhaps a recent campaign or project they've been involved

with, or some news you discovered in the press about their work;

5   Before you submit your application, have it checked by someone else and copy it, so that you can refer to it before interview.

To save time, understand how companies recruit

If you are applying to a small company (50 people or less), the way to apply may be by sending a carefully thought through and well presented letter of application, together with your CV to the boss. Spell out what your qualifications mean to make life easy for them. Get rid of any educational jargon, especially if you're applying for posts abroad. Large companies will probably have a recruitment process that includes personality tests, telephone interviews, assessment centres, interviews and more, all organised by a graduate recruitment section.

If you have to complete an application form, and send a CV with it, it is tempting to put 'see CV' on many answers, which in itself could lead to your application being deleted. Application forms give recruiters an opportunity to compare applicants, so apply the 110 per cent effort rule as opposed to 80 per cent. Apply this rule persistently and rigorously throughout the job hunting process. Remember that good manners can set you apart from other candidates.

Sumbit an outstanding application, not just an excellent one

In the recruitment process, there is one winner, i.e. the person who is selected, who will stand out over the other applicants. The person who is selected will have probably given an outstanding performance from start to finish; the others may all be excellent, but in a competitive world, there is only one winner. So if you're going to put yourself a cut above all the other applicants, you need to make yourself stand out as an outstanding candidate.

Get physical

It's a competitive world out there, so prepare yourself to fight for your part in it. Exercise daily to sharpen your mind and body – the results will be apparent from your added energy and increased focus. Minimise the rubbish you eat and drink, including alcohol. Mental agility exercises will help you improve your ability to think on your feet.

Put yourself in the recruiter's shoes

Think about what you know about the company and the sector, and the role they are recruiting for. What are they looking for? What do they want? One retail recruiter offering retail management training programmes wants: *'Customer service – it's vital for us. They need to be able to relate to the general public and to the staff who they'll be responsible for. We need to see that in a CV'.* Another employer may refer to particular skills which are essential to the job – such as a language: *'Must speak fluent Russian'* or *'Russian helpful'*. Look for clues as to what the employer is looking for.

Get practice in tests and read up on the recruitment process

If you know tests will form part of the assessment, ask your careers service for a practice run. Know what you're letting yourself in for; get used to handling questions, managing your time, and focusing on a task. The website www.prospects.ac.uk enables you to get your CV checked and talk to graduate employers and practice online personality and aptitude tests.

There are plenty of specialist books on the market regarding CVs, application forms, applying online, assessment centres and the interview process, and these are all listed under Further Information at the end of this book. Raise your standard over all the other candidates: invest a few hours in a good read. In addition, many agencies have hints and advice on their websites.

Six golden rules to kick off

1   Use a professional email address, putting your contact details at the bottom and use an appropriate header in the subject box. Address it to the right person; check their name on the company's website or by calling the switchboard.
2   Check your mobile and email regularly for messages. Recruitment can move quickly.

3   Make your application easy for recruiters to read; use bullet points, not prose. Explain your educational qualifications – spell out subjects you covered and the skills you've acquired.

4   On your CV, use a short opening statement of 30–40 words to describe your career aspirations, relating them to the role you're applying for or the company you'd like to work for. Describe the person who lies behind the CV or application form through your use of adjectives.

5   Paint the reader a picture of the scale of the projects or achievements you've worked on, using numbers, targets, deadlines, results, feedback and percentages. This will demonstrate your personal effectiveness in getting results. If your degree grants you exemptions to certain professional qualifications, say so. Be specific about the technology and computer applications you can use.

6   Be accurate with grammar and spelling. Ensure your application shows off your ability to express yourself well.

Make CVs personal and relevant to the company you're writing to

A CV should include headings for areas such as:

* Contact details (at the very top, easily spotted);
* Academic history (most recent first), pinpointing the most relevant aspects of your course to the employer and mentioning any exemptions from professional qualifications the course has given you, if relevant;
* Work experience, which outlines projects you have worked on, and gives an idea of the size of each company you have worked for;
* Overall achievements and positions of responsibility;
* Interests and leisure – keep it brief and honest;
* Personal details – for example, *'Willing to re-locate'* if you are; a clean driving licence; marital status and age (use date of birth as opposed to age in years).

Pay particular attention to the way you lay out your CV, from the font size and type to the layout and way you organise the information you wish to portray. Keep it simple, but make it look good. Limit your CV to two sides or less. Send it by email or by post on paper (good quality white A4 with no gimmicks, designs, wrinkles or coffee stains). Don't put 'Curriculum Vitae' at the top – employers know what it is. Consider the sector you want to work in. Some, such as the professions – accountancy, banking, law, etc. – expect conventional CVs. Others, such as the media, expect candidates to be more creative with attention to layout and typescript, but not pretentious.

Many applications are wasted because they are riddled with spelling errors, hard to read and poorly researched. Others get a glance and perhaps go into a 'think about while reading the rest' pile. Some are easy to read and relevant, and then one or two will make the employer think *'There's that one line which makes me sit up and think, wow – I've just got to meet this person'*.

'They want one year's experience'

If you were to add up all your work experience and put it together on your CV, you may be surprised to find that it adds up to close to a year. Can you add to that paid and unpaid experience, commissions, contracts, work simulated projects, and voluntary efforts? Put all your work experience together in a CV and put it first before your educational qualifications so that it draws the employer's attention before anything else.

Consider the skills and qualities an employer wants. For example, have you:

- Worked with a team to a tight deadline?
  The client wants this presentation tomorrow morning at 8 over breakfast.
- Managed projects, events or people?
  Such as you'll do when they recruit you.
- Initiated projects or activities?
  Let's start a careers forum online about this.
- Approached a project?
  How do you start a piece of writing like this? Take us through the process you follow.
- Taken responsibility?
  I'll find a way to do this.
- Showed resourcefulness?
  How did you fund your trip around the world?

- Showed flexibility and adaptability?
  What problems did you encounter on your travels? How did you handle them?
- Debated a point with someone and influenced them?
  (Not on the merits of going down the Union for a pint.)
- Analysed information and developed a strategy from it?
  Well, here are the figures and it looks like there are more graduates on the job market this year which means that ...
- Taken responsibility for your own learning and career development?
  I know where I'm going. I learn best by watching others and then having a go myself.
- Been driven to achieve results?
  I sold 750 tickets over the weekend in the Union for our concert – my efforts really were effective.
- Showed you can work across cultures?
  I spent six months in Kenya and two in Chile working for two voluntary organisations.

Outline relevant work and projects to date

Paint a picture of the scale of any relevant projects you've worked on, with information on the size, who it was for, what it was about, deadlines, and timescales. Include details of relevant work you've done (solo or otherwise). Choose the most relevant to the role you want. Describe any commissions you have had, together with any awards you've won, work you've sold and articles or books you may have written. Give information which shows the scale of your achievements to a potential employer, giving names, dates, and details of the work involved. If you have a website, refer the employer to it. There you can include a brief description of each work, to make them hungry enough to want to meet you.

What happens after submitting your application?

As said before, for the small or medium-sized employer, you will probably need to send a CV and accompanying letter of application and then attend for an interview.

For larger firms, kick-off may involve sending in your CV or completing an online or paper application form, or perhaps doing an online psychometric test or personality questionnaire. Many employers then run initial screening by way of short telephone interviews with candidates.

Finally, be prepared. Ask your housemates to answer the phone with greater courtesy than usual; explain that you're job hunting. Keep your details, a pen and paper by the phone, with a generic CV with your life history on it so you can quickly refer to grades you've obtained, if asked, or find information required.

Look at your potential: where do you want to be?

Where do you see yourself in five years' time? Who *do you want to become?* Increasingly, job prospects relate to the person you are and want to become (your potential), hence the heavy emphasis on psychological tests, assessment centres and even handwriting analysis in the recruitment process. It is not a good idea to say *'I'd like to be running my own company'* or *'I'll be travelling on a year off'* or *'I'd like to be in your job'*. Show ambition, but not at the expense of the interviewer, unless you're applying to a large company where there are clear ladders of progression. An employer will also want to know that you're a stayer. The recruitment process is a long and costly one, so they won't want to take on somebody who intends to leave within a year plus of joining, unless you move up their ranks.

This is a question that employers like to ask when recruiting and many job hunters think, *'Wow. I don't even know where I want to be next week! Why are these guys so hooked on this question?'* The thing to remember is that recruiting and training staff cost money and time and it's a risk. Employers need to know where your level of ambitions and drive are taking you, what your values and aspirations are and where you see yourself going. They need to look at the staff they are recruiting, to assess the spread of talents and skills they need and how you might fit and contribute to fulfilling their long-term vision, now and in the future. Large global organisations, for example, may have had to forecast their recruitment needs over a year ago. But many companies also recruit as the need arises, particularly if they are small, asking *'What could this person do for us starting from Monday?'* on the one hand, and wanting people who can grow with and contribute to the organisation on the other.

The fact that you have a degree shows your commitment to learning and developing yourself and realising your potential. An employer can see that by evidence of your conscious decision to study for a degree. They know you have the ability to learn and juggle life, study and work and progress. They can build on your strengths, weaknesses, skills, creativity, leadership abilities and management material. They can train you, probably promote you, give you a team of people to manage and expect results from you. They may provide financial and timely support for you to study towards professional examinations but they need to know that you can and will stand the pace of working relatively long hours during the weekday and studying at night. They'll look for the evidence in your application from start to finish.

More importantly, you and any potential employer need to know that you're right for each other. This is very much a two-way process. If you are not right for each other, it's far better to acknowledge it immediately. The way the organisation is structured may not enable you to meet your aspirations. Equally, if you're going on to further study, make sure you and the thing you are applying for, be it a course or role, is right for you and your long-term plans.

Interestingly, this also applies if you want to set up your own business – know where you are and where you're going, and you're more likely to get there.

Post-graduate? Consider the difference ...

If you're a post-graduate, stand back and look at the difference in you from the time you completed your undergraduate degree and now. What has changed about you and your approach as a result of your post-graduate studies? What particular skills, knowledge and breadth have you acquired from them and how would that make a difference to an employer? What difference has it made to your character and personality, your strength, direction and self-belief? How can you market that difference effectively to employers? How can you show employers that you have extra fine-tuned skills in analytical thinking, communication, self-management and motivation and in the way you look at how things are done and how other people think, work and do things? How can you avoid employers treating you as if you were an undergraduate when you know there is a difference?

Prepare to show your commercial awareness

Show you know your sector: the industry news, the movers and shakers, the main players. Where does the company fit into the sector and how does it stand out from its competitors? Why does it appeal to you over them? Can you talk about its products and services, culture and ethos? How have they grown? You want to join a company which is in the ascendent, not one which is spluttering and faltering. Who are their main clients or customers and what have their recent campaigns, products and services been? What are the hot issues of the day; who is in the headlines and why? Check share prices and read recent annual reports to see how far the company is moving towards achieving its goals or vision. Research the company through the Internet and printed press, and talk to people who know about it. Your one-page covering letter of application can make a good start in showing this off as you outline why you chose to apply to the company over its competitors. If you're applying for a voluntary or public organisation, show again that you understand how it is positioned alongside other groups.

Show how you can benefit the company and fit in

How can you demonstrate that you have researched these points:

- What is the company's mission and vision?
- How does it expect to achieve that?
- What will it need to achieve it?
- What sort of drive and personal qualities from its employees will it need to be successful?
- What can you contribute to the organisation as it works to achieve its vision?
- What does the consumer/client want?
- What are the trends and challenges facing the sector?
- What qualities will they be looking for in their employees? How can you demonstrate that you have them?
- What specific job skills does the recruiter call for that you can prove you have?
- What can you bring to the team that might be an added dimension?

- Are you ready to answer competency-based questions, giving employers a clear picture of how you approach problems and processes?
- Can you show that if they sponsor you for a professional qualification or a post-graduate course, that you've got the staying power to see it through?

Each boss or line-manager has their own criteria to meet as they recruit for a role. These may refer to particular skills which are essential to the job, such as particular IT packages, and will assess every application throughout against these criteria; they may ask the same questions of all candidates to compare their answers. Your prospective boss will look at your skills set and how they will fit with his requirements and, crucially, how you will fit in with the team.

Go into the recruitment process prepared to have fun

Most recruiters want to give you a good experience – they know you'll tell friends and family on what you thought of them. They know that if you are not in a situation where you can be yourself, they won't see the true you. The truth is that recruiters have a responsibility to take the right people on for the right roles, which is no easy task. Be prepared for the interviewer whose technique is appalling – rambling, non-stop, rude and arrogant. The website www.doctorjob.com can tell you more.

The assessment centre

Many (larger) companies use assessment centres to select their new recruits, lasting a morning or more to see how you'll cope with the demands and stresses of the job. They'll include activities such as team tasks and activities, numeracy and written tests, role-related tests (for example, creating an advert for a product if you were going into advertising), interviews and presentations, and company-specific tests. Look at each exercise from the employer's point of view. What competence or quality do you think they are looking for in the tests they have included? Focus on each one as it appears. Be prepared for the unexpected. You may be asked to present on a subject unknown to you, so that the selectors can see how you handle presenting, debating and working under pressure. Social events may not 'count' towards the assessment, but you'll be quietly watched to see how you interact. Find out what makes your potential work colleagues tick – will you want to be working with them every day under pressure? Drink an absolute minimum of alcohol. You want to be 110 per cent the next day while everyone else is at 80–90 per cent.

Attending an interview

If you go freelance or do contract work, you will need to sell yourself continually, so 'selling yourself' meetings and interviews will become second nature to you. That said, some nerves are a good sign – they show you care. Preparing for an interview or assessment day takes place at several levels:

+ Reviewing what you know about the sector you want to work in and the professional career you've chosen to follow (if relevant);
+ Researching the company using every possible resource available to you. Visit any local stores or branches. Obtain brochures and read them carefully. What impression do they give you of the company?
+ Reminding yourself of what you can contribute to that company and how it matches your career goals;
+ Practical preparations, such as dressing the part, getting there with time to spare;
+ Preparing mentally for questions you may be asked, such as *What are your strengths? Tell us about a team effort you've contributed to and what your role was. Tell us about yourself!*
+ Preparing the night before – have an early night, keep alcohol to a minimum and don't eat anything with a strong flavour such as garlic.

Get yourself in the right frame of mind. There's no point in taking baggage that spells the *'Oh poor me, I'll never get a job'* feeling. Leave it at home, put some music on which makes you feel really great en route, and focus on the task ahead. Remember, this interview is a two-way process and a chance for you to ensure that this employer is right for you, just as they need to make sure you're right for them.

A word about the *'Tell us about yourself'* question. This is not an invitation for you to recite your entire life history. Outline in a couple of sentences where you are now and where you want to be. Keep it short and throw them a couple of points they can pick up on.

Dress the part

Review your appearance. Is there anything you need to do, such as:

* Polishing shoes
* Getting shoes re-heeled
* Cleaning under your nails
* Getting a hair cut
* Making sure your suit isn't too tight or skirt too short
* Deciding what you could wear if you had to 'perform' two days running
* Looking for accessories which would enhance your image
* Not overdoing make-up, perfume or aftershave
* De-cluttering your handbag, so that you can find items easily in it
* Making sure your writing equipment – a pen and notebook – is easy to carry, professional, that your pen works and you have a standby.

Take along a copy of your CV, questions you have to ask, and any research you've found. Take directions of how to get there, and contact details of the person who organised the interview, in case you run into a problem en route. Charge your mobile phone. Account for potential problems en route when planning your journey times.

What sort of questions should you expect?

* Why us?
  Be positive! Select two or three points which made them stand out against their competitors.
* What did you think of …e.g. our brochure, website?
  Be able to back up your views. Can you compare the product or service with those of the competitors in the sector?
* What do you think you'll be doing in the first year?
  Comment on the research you've done through talking with other graduates and check your understanding of that role. Use

the opportunity to ask questions you may have about that first year and your likely career progression.

+ What is your perception of yourself?
  This is all about how you think you present yourself to people. They may ask you how you think you present yourself to them. How do you want to appear?
+ What achievement are you proudest of?
  Think up several achievements before you go in and be prepared to talk about the work you put into making them so.
+ What salary are you expecting?
  Outline the research you've done into salaries in the sector, both for new graduates and the industry as a whole. Be prepared to negotiate and remember that the added perks can affect the overall package considerably.

Remember, you're a graduate. On each point, show you've done your research and back up your answers with well thought out and cohesive answers which are clearly expressed.

Questions to ask the interviewers

Ask questions that will enable you to build up a picture of what sort of relationship you're likely to have with this employer and how your working day and week might look, both upon joining, six months after joining and then in about two to five years' time.

+ Is this a new position? If not, what is happening to the current post-holder? Are they moving up (a sign of career progression); if it is new, why has it been created?
+ Ask about the direction the company is taking – and how the company sees this post contributing to it.
+ What training and career development will be available to you? Where might you be in three to five years' time?
+ Find out what the next step is in the interview process.

Personal fit with the team

Well, you either fit, or you don't. And if you don't, it is more to do with the existing team as it is and the person the selectors want to add to it.

To get the fit right, you *may* be called back for several interviews with various team members to build up an all-round view of how you'll fit in. Take each opportunity to look closely at your potential colleagues. What would it be like making small talk by the coffee machine? Your colleagues will want to feel comfortable working with you on an assignment until three in the morning, and you'll want to feel good working alongside them.

Whatever you do, be yourself

It is exhausting to keep up any pretence, and since both you and the company are trying to find out whether the two of you are suited to one another, it is also pointless. If you rapidly come to the conclusion that this company is not for you, then look at that as a positive. Have fun. Welcome the opportunity to test yourself, and be proud that you've got this far.

Offered the post!

Congratulations! Now, take a deep breath. Is this offer really what you want? Will you be happy walking into the organisation every Monday? Can you fulfil your short and longer-term career goals with it? Is the package right?

Add up perks and benefits

Perks vary, as employers provide increasingly individualised products and services for their employees, and much depends on size and sector, but Table 7.1 below shows examples.

Perks and benefits all add up. Find out how your salary is likely to increase in the future. Bonuses will vary according to the industry you're in and how well your company – and/or you – perform. Recruitment agencies and salary surveys will tell you a great deal. Look at the kind of positions you would expect to hold in, say, three or five years' time and see what the salaries and perks are for them. How different are they to what you currently earn?

Going down the self-employed route

Make good use of professional organisations and networks to get advice, tips and tricks on how to sell your services. Above all, consider

Table 7.1

Private healthcare	Joining bonus
Pension scheme	Personal accident insurance
Holidays	A sum of money to go towards a
Profit and performance related	course of the employee's choice
bonuses	Sharesave scheme
Buy or sell extra days holiday	Season ticket loan
Flexible working hours	Disability insurance
Child care discounts	Maternity and adoption phase-back
Discounted loans and mortgages	Summer shut down
Relocation packages	Company cars
Car lease schemes/discounts	Subsidised canteen
Financial support for professional	Language training
development	Sport and adventure training
Employee helpline	Insurance
Lifestyle managers	Travel cards
Pet insurance	Payment of professional association
Discretionary bonus	membership fees
Retirement plan	Work-wear
Social activities	

yourself as a business – you are – and promote and sell yourself as such. Think back to your work experience days. How did companies you worked with portray themselves? What can you emulate from their approach?

Consider where you're heading financially

What do you want to achieve financially through your language skills? Set yourself financial targets. Your bank or a business adviser can help you but you should have a clear idea of your costs, including equipment, your own pay, taxes and insurance, how much items will cost to produce, and what you'll charge for your products and services. And look at the examples of perks listed earlier in Table 7.1, Which are important to you long-term and immediately? A bank loan may keep you watered, fed, sheltered and clothed.

How are you going to sell your work?

As the freelancer or business owner, whatever it is that you have to sell needs to be out there, selling itself and your talent; and as soon as it is finished, you need to start work on another and get that out in front of the public eye, too. You need to take a commercial viewpoint.

You need to find out which marketing and PR methods work for you and your business. Think laterally and your potential market will expand. And always, always display your contact details. If you choose to have a website as a translator or interpreter, visit the website www.webpack.webserved.co.uk/ which is a new marketing service for linguists and set up with small businesses, freelancers and those starting-up in mind.

You need to find out which marketing and PR methods work for you and your business. There are many methods, such as:

- forming a strategic alliance with hotels, tourist offices, other translators and interpreters who cover different languages, virtual assistants, with letters to their clients on your behalf explaining that your work will be showing;
- if you're a translator or interpreter, form an alliance with virtual assistants who perform PA responsibilities for small employers from home (www.iava.org.uk) – you can complement each other's services;
- write new releases for the local press on items which are relevant to your sector; include your contact details at the bottom.

Think laterally and your potential market will expand. And always, always display your contact details.

Summary action points

Once you've started sending applications or taking steps towards your proposed first career move after your degree:

1   Keep a record of what you're sending out and when; this will help you to ascertain whether you're doing enough towards your goal.
2   Assess what is working particularly well and build on that.
3   Obtain feedback where you can to help you improve your performance the next time.
4   Get involved in a couple of things in life other than careers and job hunting to help keep a balance in your day and week.

Chapter 8

What's stopping you? Make it happen!

Frequently in life, things seem to take far too long to go our way. We're waiting for that great job, or know that there isn't going to be one in the region we are in. We're waiting for a lucky break. But all too often, *we* are the people who stop ourselves getting what we want in life.

There are varying scenarios that befall us. For example, you can fall into a rut. You feel that you need a boost with the firepower of a space shuttle to get out of it, followed by a long sustained blast of persistent rocket fuel-type effort. This doesn't just happen in your career, but in relationships with people; perhaps the excitement has gone out of a relationship and you need a super-boost of impetus and excitement to bring it back to life. Perhaps your ability to be spontaneous in life has been overtaken by a preference for the known, safe and comfortable.

It may be that the situation you're in needs one bold, decisive step to get to where you want to be, but you feel like taking that step is like being asked to ski down the steepest, highest most icy slope. You just need to push yourself over the edge and set off, but it's making that first push which freezes you. At this point, we often fear failure and of looking like a fool in front of others – but we also fear success. We procrastinate from making that call, for fear of being turned down, rejected – but what if we succeed? How will we handle the changes in life that will invariably follow? Will we cope with them?

And then we make glorious plans, and life gets in the way. Family problems, a friend in trouble, illness, death, redundancy, changes thrust upon us, rows ... they all combine to be the reasons why we are where we are.

And sometimes, it seems that we aren't getting anywhere or at least where we want to be as quickly as we wish. Maybe we're waiting for that magic breakthrough – selected at interview, obtaining funding for that post-graduate course, securing an introduction and follow-up meeting with an employer you really want to work for, having a business idea while in the shower. We're waiting, confident that these things will happen one day. If we don't stay on top of things and create the right environment and conditions for success, we will probably wait a long time.

It's at times like these that your university days can seem a distant memory, and the weight of debt around your neck heavier than ever.

Don't forget what you went to university for!

If your career plans are taking an age to come to fruition, it can be really frustrating to see all those successful people at work who didn't go to university who say, *'Well, university wasn't for me, and now I'm a millionaire several times over'*. It can be easy to fall into the trap of blaming others for your current situation, thinking and saying things like *'Well, the school pushed us into it'*, and *'My parents thought it would be a good idea'*.

Five survival tips are:

1   Recognise that there are gifted people who chose not go to university but who have made it up the ladder by another route – people reach their potential in their own way and time; what matters is that they get there.

2   Keep everything in perspective – you have as much chance of succeeding as they do.

3   Learn from them.

4   Recall what you got out of your university days. No one can ever take them away from you, or your degree.

5   Focus on where you want to be. Review the progress you've made so far and assess how far you've moved towards achieving your main goals. Identify what else you need to do.

Dig deeper into your resources

Whether you fall into a rut or you need to take that one decisive, courageous step, there will always be stages in your life where you need to get tough with yourself and dig deeper within you for the resources you need to achieve the result you want. These resources usually come from within us: energy, focus, clarity of vision and action required, determination, an ability to go out there and get on with it. You've done it before, when you chose to apply to university – and then when you packed up and left home to head out there. It is *the* time to look afresh into the way you spend your time and energy and to get any unwanted stuff out of the way, such as anything that pulls you down.

Strengthen your resolve

You can choose to change your attitude, approach and luck, and you'll have subconsciously done so many times in your life when you felt good about what you were doing, things were going well, and you were on course for where you were heading. You may not have been aware that you were doing them. Since then, you probably picked up some bad habits, so it's a good time to make sure they aren't holding you back.

Dump the 'I'll try'. Trying isn't the answer

You can train yourself to think positivly and talk positivly by watching your language. If you're planning to do something, and think *'I'll try to do this before lunch tomorrow'*, then in fact you're unlikely to do it. Think *'I will do this tomorrow before lunch'*, and you inject a whole new energy into your focus and you're far more likely to get the thing done. Watch your language for a morning and listen for positive and negative statements. If you're talking more negatively than positively, that will be affecting your mood and manner. You can change that by simply talking more positively and changing your state and the way you're feeling.

What message are you taking on board?

Sometimes we don't help ourselves. If we're feeling down, and we watch a depressing television programme in which people are rowing and living mediocre lives, that's going to make us feel worse. If we listen to a piece of music we love and which makes us feel great and fantastic, then our approach to life changes. Aim for the positive and get a lift from it. Assess the information you receive in any format, dump the negative, work with the positive and strive for the possible and realistic.

Are you caught up in unhelpful patterns of thinking and behaviour?

Examples include criticising yourself, imposing limits or boundaries on the opportunities before you. It involves giving yourself excuses for failing before you start, spending more time on socialising than job hunting, so not giving your career the prominence in your life that it deserves. Perhaps you're being too influenced by listening to generalisations from people who don't know what they're talking about; or you're not applying any creativity to your problem to find a solution. Either way, you make the choice whether to take those on board and listen to them, or not.

Acknowledge there's a misunderstanding by others of what graduates can do for them

This is particularly the case in the SME market, where many bosses cannot keep up-to-date with all the changes in education at any level, unless they are parents. So make it easy for them. Pay particular attention to your work experience when you write your CV and paint as clear a picture as you can for them of what you can do with clear examples.

Use your problem-solving skills

What can you do to solve the problem?

1   Identify a problem or issue you have now, such as finding that first right role, making your business work, or paying off your student debts.
2   Revise where you are now with the problem and identify the solution you want.
3   What is happening right now?
    ◆   What are you doing which is working for you?
    ◆   *You've tried everything?* Okay, ask yourself:
        ◆   What exactly have you tried?
        ◆   How often have you tried it?

- When specifically?
- How much time did you spend on it? How carefully did you do it?
- What is working well? What isn't?
- Look back over the last seven days. What did you do on each of those seven days to tackle the problem? If you only spent an hour on Monday and Wednesday doing something, you cannot expect to solve it.

If you learn from this exercise that you're only spending two hours a week making new friends, but that friendship is important to you, then something in your week needs to change. You may need to sacrifice something else to allow room for the change to happen. If you want to work on your portfolio but only devote three hours a week to it, and four evenings to going out with friends, well, your social life is going to look pretty good; your portfolio won't. Devote four evenings to your portfolio, and that fifth evening spent with friends really will feel well deserved.

4   What extra resources and skills do you need to make the change happen? Table 8.1 below gives hints! Where will you get them from?

5   Look for new solutions.
  - Brainstorm every single thing you can think of that you might do to change the situation to make it just the way you want it to be.
  - What one thing do you need to do differently to get the results you need?
  - What else could you do?
  - What other ways could you approach the issue?
  - What would you advise a friend to do?
  - Who do you know who is where you want to be now?
  - What help and advice could they offer you?

Table 8.1

Extra	Contacts
Skills	Knowledge
Time	Experience
Energy	Influence
Qualifications	Materials
Opportunities	

 + Who might have experienced the same problem before and could help you unblock where you are now by acting as a mentor to you?
   + If you're running your own company, what could you do to market yourself?
6 Finally, identify the actions you are prepared to take and when you're going to take them. Pinpoint any support you'll need and identify where you can get that from.

Focus on what you can change

Do something about the things you can change and don't waste time worrying about the things you cannot. When you look at the graduate recruitment market and your life after graduation, identify the things you can influence. If you're self-employed, look at the way you organise your resources because you can influence the way you access and use them.

Pinpoint the missing angle which, once added, could lead to success

What do you need to do to turn your current position into a success and get to where you want to be? For example, you could consider:

1 Working for employers who naturally take on students with one or two years' experience after university. Why not find out how this route into the workplace would help you? Here your alumni associations with your old university could be invaluable.
2 Moving into an allied profession for a couple of years and then shifting track later, either in your own country or abroad.
3 Relocating now to where the opportunities are – which could be further afield than you like.
4 Working part time or on short-term stints until you find the right position. Go freelance!
5 Discussing your situation with relevant professional organisations; how flexible are the rules and regulations governing entry to and qualification for membership?
6 Starting your own business. There are lots of opportunities and programmes around for graduates who have business ide-

as, so find out what support and finance might be on offer and brainstorm that business idea!

7   Joining forces with fellow students from your course and brainstorm the issue together. What could you do collectively to turn the current situation into an opportunity?

Boost your creativity into solving problems and looking for opportunities. Get friends to help you brainstorm, and that way you're also tapping into their knowledge and creativity.

What practical steps can you take?

There could be *practical* steps you need to take to blow barriers away. Let's look at some of them.

Identify your skills gaps

Look at anything which may boost your employability. Would a particular skill boost your chances in landing the role you crave? Does the agency you've signed up with offer any particular training courses which you could benefit from? If you're temping, talk to your consultant about how you can strengthen your chances to get the job you want. Could you sign up for a professional qualification, for example, while you're looking for the job you want?

In many cases, it won't be your skills which are at a loss. It will be your experience or own organisational skills which are missing. Pinpoint where the gap is between where you are and where you want to be and work out what you need to do to fill it. That gap could consist of particular skills or knowledge.

While waiting for a response...

One of the traps writers tend to fall into is that they will send out a proposal to a publisher or editor and then wait for a response. What they should be doing is congratulating themselves for getting a proposal out, and then heading straight back to their desks to work on the next one. Don't fall into the same trap. As soon as you've finished work on one application, start on the next.

Keep working at your craft or career, whatever it is. There will be days when you wonder how on earth you can keep going and when you'll get your lucky break, especially if you're combining your language work with another job to keep the money coming in. Stand back and take a long-term approach but ensure that you work continually towards your end goal. Continually add to your experience, your network and your CV. Get your skills and talents out on show; don't tuck them away where no one can see them. Offer to do something for a local charity or business for free – you can talk about at interview and you can show that you understand the importance of talking to the client and taking their views on board, that you have kept the bottom-line in mind and worked with a team to see an idea through the conception stage and on to completion.

What specialist help is about to help you overcome any barriers you're hitting?

Many groups with special needs now have their own support networks, such as those who have had cancer or heart problems, mature workers, ex-offenders, those returning to the work after a break, people with disabilities, those with learning difficulties, asylum seekers, ethnic minorities, women – the list is simply endless. There are websites set up to help you, such as SKILL at www.skill. org.uk for students and graduates with a disability.

How well are you promoting yourself?

Think about the way you're selling yourself in terms of your approach, enthusiasm and passion for the industry. You need to show yourself as a person who can be trusted in the way you handle people and situations. Construct whole sentences, rather than using texting language that you'd send to your friends and family. Do not call people 'mate,' 'darling' or any other form of endearment. They are not your 'mates.'

Some simple do's and don'ts now follow. Patronising? No, they are merely included because of employers' comments regarding the lack of basic social skills and manners in many graduates. Practice a warm firm handshake with your friends, looking people in the eye. Keep your shoulders back and square and your head up. You can practice this with strangers you meet in everyday life. When you meet new people, use this handshake and smile. Drop the grunt; you're a graduate: sell yourself as such. Show yourself to be a positive, can do person. Leave the moods at home. We all get black days but there is no need to bring them to work. Do not whine about your current situation or blame past employers, teachers or anyone else for the state you are in. Be positive about going to university. You chose to do it and you gained from it, even though it may not seem like it right now.

Common concerns

I've just got a 2:2 ...
You're lucky. I've only got a third ...

Well, many employers are stipulating that yes, they do want a 2:1 or above and some are quite adamant that they won't consider anyone with lower than that. But there are plenty of good employers out there who *will* and your task now is to focus not on what you cannot change but what you can do and influence to get your foot in the door. Focus on what you *can* offer in the way of key skills, personal qualities and drive and motivation – things you can promote and sell to an employer who will want to know how you can contribute in the future. Could you work for that employer in a couple of years' time after getting some relevant experience behind you?

What about my age?

If you omit your age from your CV or application altogether, employers will wonder even more about your age. Use your date of birth (not your age e.g. 44 years) – it takes longer to work out so people are less likely to bother until later – and put it towards the end of your CV so that the recruiter can be excited about what you have to offer first. But, there are plenty of good things about being a mature worker and you should show that you mix easily with younger people (not mentioning children or grandchildren) in working situations, that you believe you can learn from each other, and get your image checked to make sure you look smart, crisp and fresh. Emphasise your work experience and the good points about maturity; many employers find mature staff more reliable. Show, too, that you can handle change well and that you're not stuck in your ways.

Being successful abroad

The key to success with a move abroad is to immerse yourself totally into the culture and to meet as many locals as you can. If you stick with people of your own nationality, you might as well have stayed at home. Learn a little of the language before you go, at least enough to be able to say some pleasantries; if you can, talk to people who've worked there so that you know what to expect and what the differences will be. Take pictures of your family and friends to show new friends that you're human too. Enrol in a language school when you arrive to boost your skills. Read the local papers to find out what's happening and observe local customs and, in particular, dress. Ultimately, you want to win people over rather than alienate them. Watch, listen and observe and see what you can learn from people.

Learn from failure

If you're going to succeed in work, either as an entrepreneur or an employee, you need to be tough and tenacious, and to learn from failure. Two-thirds of all start ups fail in the first three years, for example, but many successful entrepreneurs point out that failure can be a tremendous learning tool. Failures give up their dreams and goals. They don't learn from the experience because they don't even try to see where they went wrong. They usually fall into the blame culture. Winners and successes may fail, but they learn from their failures and take the experience forward to build future successes.

Analyse failure, and you move forward. View it as part of the learning curve of life, and you'll come out much stronger for it. The tough times in life show you that you have what it takes to survive and come out of situations on top. As you get older, you realise how much you've grown from all those difficult times in work and personal lives. We all hit rough patches in life, like an aircraft going through turbulence, but we usually come out of it all the stronger for it. When you look back on something in this context, if you learn from an experience, you can hardly describe it as failure.

Don't take failure personally

If you didn't get that much cherished job you wanted, perhaps it simply wasn't meant to be – maybe someone else was simply a better fit for the post and the company. Take your 'failure' with you in the next interview and you won't win any friends. Invest in a punch bag or get aggressive in the gym instead, get feedback if you can and review your performance yourself.

Ten survival steps to coping with failure

1   Have faith in yourself – there will be that perfect position for you somewhere out there, but you need to know what you're looking for. Keep focused and keep trying.
2   Keep knocking at doors. Get help and support around you, both experts in the field and your friends and family.
3   Ask for advice on turning those potential applications into sure bets.
4   Look for new strategies.
5   Keep a sense of perspective.
6   Don't turn to comfort eating, drink or drugs. It won't make change anything. Keep healthy.
7   Learn from those who have failed but picked themselves up and gone on to be successful.
8   Obstacles in our way are often our unwillingness to say 'no' to people, or our belief in ourselves as much as anything real or physical.
9   Push yourself out of your boundary zone at every opportunity you get. You'll be surprised how much you can achieve.
10 Live life differently if you can. A fresh approach works wonders and avoids your getting stuck in a rut.

Self-employed and ...

Someone's pinched my idea!

If you're going to create and implement designs or ideas or anything of that ilk, you'll want copyrights, patents and trademarks. Protect your own ideas and designs by making full use of the support available to you, such as:

- Institute of Trade Mark Attorneys
  www.itma.org.uk
- Usability Professionals' Association
  www.upassoc.org
- Own It
  www.own-it.org
- The Writers Copyright Association
  www.wcauk.com/
  This body protects the rights of writers:
- Webmasters Copyright Association
  www.wmcaglobal.org/

Finally, the Charter on Intellectual Property promoted a new user-friendly way of handing out intellectual property rights in 2005, written by an international group of artists, scientists, lawyers, politicians, academics and business experts.

Access to finance

Apart from the obvious organisations to try, such as professional bodies and trade organisations, don't forget to tap into the various initiatives which may be taking part in your country or region to encourage growth and regeneration.

Needing help on a particular aspect of your journey?

Certainly in the UK, the creative and cultural industries sector is enjoying huge growth in many parts of the country. A consequence of that is that many cluster groups develop, by which artists and writers in the broadest sense of the word can meet with colleagues and other like-minded professionals, share best practice and benefit from each other's experience, expertise and network. Many of these will have individuals you can tap into for expert help and advice. These vary in the way in which they are organised and in the help they can give you. BusinessLink's network can help you, firstly, to set up your own business, and secondly, to grow the business, with help and information in areas such as exploiting your ideas, employing people, health and safety, premises, international trade, finance, grants and guidance on the rules and regulations applying to businesses in the creative industries sector.

Not getting the commissions?

If you're running your own business but you're not achieving the sales you want, think about what is working for you and what is not. Contact people who have decided not to buy or pursue your product or service, and ask for some feedback. Is there anything in your sales pitch which did not endear them to your sale? What could you have done differently to achieve a different outcome? If there was nothing, were you looking in the right place for clients to start with, or pricing it properly? Obtain business advice, either from local business advisers or specific industry bodies.

Persist and persevere, but learn and listen to where you're going wrong and then put it right next time.

Summary action points

Identify barriers and obstacles and then do something about them through creative thinking.

1   Identify what barriers and obstacles you have ahead of you which may hinder you achieving your goals.
2   Now pinpoint as many ways to tackle them as you can.
3   Identify the one which will work best for you and do it.

Chapter 9

Moving on ... Your future

No matter who you work for, careers and businesses need nurturing and loving care just like any relationship in life. If you look after them, devote time and energy to them and focus on them, they will blossom. You need to give your career loving care, or it will degenerate into just a job.

First, though, you need to walk before you can run

So you've signed up, started work, and you know you're expected to hit the ground running and adjust to the workplace culture as quickly as you can. What can you do to make this easier for yourself?

Ask if you can go into the office and spend a couple of hours meeting colleagues before your official start date, a bit like a Freshers' week at work condensed into a few hours. This will give you a chance to find out where things are and get familiar with the area. Take a good look at your colleagues-to-be to check the dress code, and work out what you're going to wear each day in that first week. Make sure it's clean, pressed and that there are no buttons hanging off. Organise your meals for the week, so that you don't have to think about what to eat at night or buy food on the way home.

However nervous you are, keep smiling. Most people recall what it was like on their first day; they will want to put you at ease. Put in a sustained effort, so don't burn yourself out by being overly friendly in the first few hours. As you meet people, offer a friendly firm handshake and a smile. If you're working for a large company, ask for a buddy who can help and guide you if you have questions about the place, someone you can turn to for advice and information. Talk to people by the coffee machine and join them for lunch if you can.

They are human, after all, and you're hoping for a relatively long association with them as friends and colleagues.

Find out about the company policy regarding mobiles and personal emails; and before you put any information online, such as blogs, consider how it could be used. Keep your own counsel; don't shoot your mouth off. Pick your confidantes and true work friends with care. Confidential means just that.

Starting work in any company can be frustrating for a few weeks. You want to prove yourself and settle in. Yet being in a new work environment is just like being in a country you've never visited before, with lots to learn: how the computer system works, and whether there is an intranet; whose approval you need for what; who the key decision makers are; and what people do at lunch time. You'll also learn who is who, what is where, and try to remember names and what people do.

Make an impact!

Eight ways to do this are:

1   Be friendly without being gushingly so. Don't call people 'mate'. They are not your mates (yet); they are work colleagues;
2   Listen and learn how things work before you dive in with comments; find out the history behind something which looks strange to you before you make suggestions;
3   Ask people questions about themselves and their role. '*What do you do? How long have you been here?*' It's a great way to learn who does what;
4   Be willing to stay late to get things done;
5   Double-check your work for accuracy;
6   Prove you're a safe pair of hands to be trusted and a team player who fits in.
7   Be ready to begin at the bottom and use the opportunity to learn as much as you can about the way the organisation functions.
8   Get social. Hang about and talk to people, have a coffee or drink with them.

As well as working, there's the added stress of handling full-time work five days a week, and doing all those small but essential tasks needed to keep life ticking along smoothly. If you spend eight hours a day sleeping (56 hours a week) and nine hours a day working, including the commute to work, that leaves you with 67 hours a week to do your admin, paying bills and banking; laundry and ironing, cleaning and shopping, cooking, eating and washing up, personal hygiene and, more occasionally, check ups with the doctor, dentist, hygienist and gynaecologist, and taking the car to the garage for an MOT. You'll also want time to enjoy activities such as socialising, catching up with old mates, remembering your parents, leisure hobbies, exercise, having weekends away and that all important 'me' down time to relax and re-charge your batteries. On top of all that, you may have enrolled for further learning or work towards a professional qualification.

Studying for professional qualifications or a part-time postgraduate degree?

If you've decided to study for professional qualifications, talk to your current employer to find out what support they can give you. This may take a number of forms such as study leave or financial support, perhaps paying for all or part of the course, or your study materials or examinations. When approaching the subject, look to show how far the studies will boost your effectiveness on the job and benefit your employer, so that you present a 'win–win' situation.

Professional bodies should have information online regarding continued professional development, including which institutions are accredited to offer which course. Some have mentors who can help you with your time management and learning organisation, both essential ingredients to success.

Work out the time which is best for you to study. The time could be late at night, in the early hours of the morning or at the start of a new day. You know when you work best and at your most effective. It requires real motivation and dedication to do this. There will be many occasions when you just feel like switching off and doing something totally different or even nothing at all. Get advice from those who've been there before to learn from those who've done it. Find a quiet place and time to study and reward yourself afterwards. Above all, keep the reason you're studying for the qualifications at the forefront of your mind, because it will keep you going when times get tough.

It's not working out!

If you think things aren't going well as you try to settle into a new job, give it time. Ask for feedback on your performance. Can you pinpoint what it is that is not quite right? Do you need more support from your boss or line-manager? At the least, view this role as a stepping stone to something better. It can take a couple of attempts to get the match of employer and role right; many employers appreciate that. In fact, some even deliberately take on graduates a couple of years after their degree, with the understanding that their first post may not have lived up to their expectations or worked out. But think before you move. You don't want to acquire a reputation as a job hopper.

So what happens next?

There are a number of 'what' and 'where' and 'how' questions here. What have you achieved so far, and where do you see your career going next? Are there any potential barriers or obstacles which might hinder your progress? Can you acquire extra skills to give you more openings in the employment market? If you are working for an industry which thrives on employing freelancers, you will need to be particularly pro-active in networking and promotion yourself. Some websites have advice for people who have been made redundant or pages to offer support to freelancers. Within industries, there are more and more 'sub-groups' around delving in niche areas which help people work towards enhancing their skills and knowledge, particularly for those who are self-employed.

A dogged, persistent effort is essential to take you to career success, in which these skills will be essential:

* Self-awareness
  Knowing your strengths, weaknesses, passions, ambitions, values and needs
* Self-promotion
  Raising your profile in the organisation and sector
* Exploring and creating opportunities
  Being pro-active in taking responsibility for your own career development
* Decision making and action planning

Making informed, decisive decisions that will take you in the right direction and working out what needs to be done and when
- Coping with uncertainty
  Dealing with redundancy, restructuring, new clients, new to-morrows
- Transfer of skills
  Thinking laterally and broadly, applying the commonalities to the workplace and life
- Self-belief and confidence
  Yes, you can do it!
- Willingness to learn
  New products, new technology, new skills
- Commitment/dependability
  Everyone knowing you're a safe pair of hands, and management and your own staff trusting you
- Self-motivation
  Having drive and enthusiasm, and taking the initiative
- Co-operation
  People wanting to have you on board their team
- Knowledgeable about new developments in the field
  Showing that you're up-to-date.

Plot and plan your next steps effectively, pinpointing the learning and experiences you will need to get to the next stage, especially if you are in a lower level position than you had hoped for after leaving university. Set a long-term goal and break it down into manageable steps. Keep these at the forefront of your mind. While everyone else sleeps and parties, work at your goal. You'll soon climb the career ladder through your own dogged determination, persistence and perseverance. Failures in life give up. Winners persist.

Getting promoted

If you want to move up, plan for it and prepare the ground! For instance, if you get the chance to train any new staff or take responsibility for a group, do it; you can show off your management potential. Ensure your team knows what is expected of them and treat them all fairly and equally. When you delegate, check that people know what needs to be done, by when, and ask if they need any help. Explain why the task is important. Listen to their feedback and questions. Show how effective you are and tell your boss about the results you're getting. Watch the behaviours of those higher up and ask them what has worked for them.

Smooth the path to promotion

Make sure you have a regular review to assess your performance and how you're progressing. Out of the office, ask yourself if you're on track to achieve your career goals in the timescale you want with your employer. Review the way you work – how can you handle your work-load more effectively and time efficiently while maintaining or improving your performance? Ensure you understand what any new role is about and what it contributes to the organisation's vision, and ensure that your team is properly trained and motivated to achieve the results expected of them. As you progress up the ladder, wear a managerial hat rather than a technical one, and take a higher helicopter view looking at the bigger picture. Delegate where you can, developing those you supervise through coaching, mentoring and one-to-one training. Assess whether you need any extra skills or qualifications to progress your path, such as an MBA or post-graduate or professional studies. And consider how changes at work could provide you with new opportunities.

A strong network right across a company could smooth your path into new roles and it will raise your profile. Get on a committee so that other people can see how you perform. Keep up-to-date with everything that is going on in your sector and in your clients' sector. Be the first to know. Finally, dress for the role you aspire to, not the role you're in.

Are you working for a small company?

Sit down with the boss every six months or so to review your progress and the results you have achieved. Then talk about your career progression. Look to build up your skills and experience – can you take on more, for extra reward? Is there a project you can get into which will give you the experience you need?

And outside the office ...

Networking is as important outside a company as you climb the career ladder as it is in it. Many senior managers and professionals are recruited through recruitment agencies, head-hunters and search companies. These companies receive assignments from organisations which have roles to fill. Headhunters will call around their contacts in the industry to see if they know of anyone who might fit the bill. Someone in your network may think of you ...

Know your worth

Prior to your reviews, find out what the industry pays someone with your experience and qualifications, but don't forget that perks can make a huge difference to the overall package. Many agencies have salary reviews on their websites. Pull all your evidence together of what you've contributed to the company, plus your research on salary and put your case forward for a rise if you want one. Don't expect to get an immediate answer and don't be surprised if the answer is no, but be prepared to negotiate. Perhaps the company will pay for you to undertake further studies instead of having a salary increase. There are ways and means to enhance your overall package.

Make the most of your professional body

Many professional bodies have different types of membership depending on the stage you are at in your career. Are you raising your level of membership to match your experience? Can you get involved in a working group to boost your network and knowledge and influence the direction it takes, or get involved in your region and give something back to those young professionals coming through?

Those who put persistent effort into job hunting will succeed in securing the job they want

The problem with acquiring lower level jobs for the sake of paying off your debts is that they can quickly become long term. Of course you may feel there are no alternatives in your area – *'There wasn't anything going, so I took this'*. And don't forget that you can also work for companies over the Internet, which may be a viable alternative. Look at your skills and see how you can put them to work. The graduate who is most active and really thinks about his or her job search will be the most successful. If you put more into planning your annual holiday than your career, you can expect to have a fabulous four to six weeks in your life every year. And the rest of it may not live up to your aspirations and expectations.

Continue to train and learn

You'll need to learn both in and outside work throughout your life. Many people do not take up training because they don't have enough time, or their family and personal commitments prevent them from doing so; or they don't see the point. View training as an investment, which boosts your employability.

As a graduate, you're more likely to ask for training because you are used to identifying your own training and learning needs and making sure they are met. Your university studies will have taught you how to learn through many methods, which will prepare you well for training at work. You can learn informally, by reading books and articles, taking correspondence courses, accessing learning materials on the Internet and also more formally for a qualification. You can also learn by being shown how to do things and then practising them, or through one-to-one training and coaching sessions with a manager or boss. Identify where your skills gaps are and what you need to do to close that gap. Think about skills which will give your company or your own performance an added dimension and get you ahead of the rest.

Continued Professional Development (CPD)

The new Sector Skills Councils in the UK are working to ensure employers have the skills they need in the future, and that education and training systems match the requirements employers have. Visit professional bodies to find out what is on offer to:

1   Update your job-related skills and technical knowledge;
2   Boost your transferable skills and ability to handle people;
3   Develop your business – many organisations have helpful workshops and training for the self-employed;
4   Prove you're up-to-date – you can add courses to your CV, for example, when applying for work with a new company.

Essential CPD

It may be essential for you to continue with your learning and training after you've achieved professional status on an annual basis. This helps keep you up-to-date with new technologies, skills, developments and knowledge and you should discuss your needs with your employer or contact the most relevant professional body to assess what you need to do to meet this commitment. Invest time in training and continued development – it's a great way to put fresh impetus into your work and career and will help ensure continued career progression. Plan your CPD well ahead in the year to ensure that you meet any necessary targets and can truly select something which will enhance your learning.

Identify the training and learning you need to get to where you want to be or to do your role more effectively. If you work with languages, you will need to do this on several levels, such as taking your language expertise to the next level and keeping abreast of trends, terminology and changes in the sector you are most closely associated with. Set yourself career goals, especially if you are in a lower level position than you had hoped for when acquiring a degree, or if you work for a small company. Break long-term goals down into manageable steps. While everyone else sleeps and parties, work at your goal. You'll soon climb the career ladder through your own dogged determination and persistence but you need to be clear about where you're heading. Track your progress.

Look to see what is going on in your sector

Visit the main professional bodies to find out whether there are any one-day courses or meetings with speakers which will be of interest. Examples from the Institute of Linguists include a one-day course for professional interpreters on becoming a court interpreter or business interpreter.

What about an MBA?

If you're considering doing an MBA, contact the Association of MBAs (see Useful Addresses at the end of this book) which represents the international MBA community: its students, graduates, schools, businesses and employers. The Association promotes the MBA as a leading management qualification and aims to encourage management education at post-graduate level to create highly competent professional managers. MBAs benefit those students who want to be effective at a strategic level. There's plenty of opportunity to share ideas and experiences with students. The MBA provides an invaluable opportunity to develop your career, with a portfolio of managerial tools and techniques as well as the 'softer' skills needed to succeed as a manager such as an entrepreneurial spirit, dedication, commitment and professionalism. In some sectors, the MBA is a must have and it will help your chances of success, whether you decide to go on and work for someone else or to set up business on your own.

Leaving your current employer

Employers expect that you have a fine brain and that you've been taught to use it and develop it. You know how to access information, how to analyse it and draw conclusions from it. Challenge your brain and creative thinking processes at every single opportunity you get, because it's like an elastic band: the more you stretch it, the more you'll get out of it. At university, you pushed your brain out of its comfort zone, both academically and in living the experience. This was why, for most people, university is a great experience. The unhappy people at work are those who are bored, because they've stopped pushing themselves and expect someone else to take the responsibility to make their career dreams happen. They've stopped learning, growing and developing.

Keep taking stock

If you're not on a professional career with a specific path, it's even more important to stop and take stock from time to time. Without such a step, you'll be like a ship's captain without a chart.

Seven point plan to taking action

1   Stop.
2   Consider where you are in relation to where you're heading.
3   Does your original goal need amending or changing in any way?

4   What do you need to do more of to boost your progress?
5   Who do you need to help you?
6   What steps do you need to take?
7   When will you take them?

Before you even think about handing in your notice, ensure that there are absolutely no other opportunities at your current company. Consider what you have done to create opportunities for expanding your role and taking on new projects and responsibilities? What is right with the job you have now? Often there's plenty we like about our work, and it's the bits we don't like that we tend to focus on and gripe about.

Now look forward. Have your ambitions got lost in the current role you're in? Before you decide whether you can achieve them with your current employer, talk to your boss and/or human resources and put an action plan together to help you get back on track. If your current employer cannot meet your future aspirations, *then* research a move to another organisation or setting up business on your own. Get the new deal signed before giving in your notice. Be discreet, and don't work at your CV in work time on a work PC. Use the internet and specialist agencies, your network and company websites to help you find that next right move.

Relocating abroad

If we choose to work abroad, many of us would like to think that we can go back to our homes after years away. Keep an eye on developments in your home country to make sure that time spent away doesn't prevent you from returning to your home country of birth, buying a house, settling down or anything else. When you're looking at any financial provision for your future, check to see what the taxation implications are if you move about. How will working abroad affect any pension due to you later in life, for example, be it state or private? A good accountant with international experience should be able to help you. Shop around to get the best deal you can.

So you've set up your own business and want to go for growth?

As you grow, delegate as much as you can, so that you're free to focus on the business. One possibility is to hire a virtual assistant, whom you would pay by the hour. Visit the website www.iava.org. uk to find out more.

Consider these questions:

* What have you achieved to date?
* What are your strengths, weaknesses, opportunities and threats?
* Where do you see your business going in the next year? The next five years?
* What extra resources do you need, e.g. time, money, equipment?
* Who can help you with that?
* What new products or services are you creating/innovating?
* What extra staff if any do you need and how will you find and employ them?
* What are you doing to build your niche and brand?
* What are your financial targets for the year?
* How much time are you devoting to business planning?
* What can you outsource, leaving yourself to focus on developing the business?
* What are you doing to get feedback from your customers to enhance the prospect of repeat business?
* Which marketing methods are proving to be most effective?
* What three new ways can you think of to market your business?
* What three new things can you think of to surprise and delight existing customers?
* Which comes first: business or lifestyle?

Look at the examples of perks listed earlier on page 120. Which are important to you long term and immediately? What do you need to do to make them happen? Many of them won't be critical, but you could incorporate them into your working life with a different slant. Would you benefit from a monthly session with a business coach or mentor? Do you need a loan from the bank to keep you watered, fed, sheltered and clothed?

Looking to leave the day job behind

You may be working in the day to get some money coming in and tackling your 'real' job at night, hoping to resign when you hit a breakthrough. If this sounds like you, make sure your 'night' job is honestly going places by asking the following questions:

- What have you achieved overall so far?
- What is working well?
- Where can you create more time in your day?
- Where do you want to be in six months' time?
- What will you need to do to make that happen?
- Who can help you further?
- What do you need to do to move your business to the next stage?
- How can you add value to your products and services so as to bring in extra income and enable you to focus more on the business and reduce the time you're spending on the day job?

Finally, keep your bank informed of how things are going. It's better to talk to them when problems are small rather than wait until the day when they have grown out of all proportion.

Don't forget to tap into useful resources!

The Institute of Linguists (www.iol.org.uk) has a number of links through to various sites relating to languages, three of which are:

www.ilovelanguages.com

A huge catalogue of language-related internet resources, with reviews of products, jobs available, conferences, links, commercial help, teaching and more, online dictionaries and translators.

www.thebigword.com

A translation services company, offering services in document translation, web translation and localisation, interpreting, for permanent, temporary or contract work. They work in almost 80 countries.

www.eslworldwide.com/

ESL Worldwide, a community and job search site for teachers of languages, with a job search facility, country profiles and statistics from overseas correspondents in Africa, Asia, South America, Europe, Middle East and Australasia, North America and the Caribbean and Central America, plus information on insurance and teacher training. The site is also shortly to have its own travel service.

Flexibility and adaptability go a long way to making the most of life

You may be merrily making your way through your career and then something happens which changes everything for you at a stroke.

Ten events which could change your life and your career

1   You meet your future partner; and life is never the same;
2   Your create a baby and parenthood is on the way;
3   You hit on a business or social idea which, if implemented, will really make a difference;
4   You or one or your relatives or a friend falls seriously ill or has an accident and needs special care and love; plus it makes you re-think;
5   You get head-hunted;
6   A major world event makes you rethink life;
7   You volunteer for a cause you believe in;
8   You decide to live abroad;
9   You win the lottery;
10 You take the decision that you want to live a higher quality life and set about doing just that.

Summary action points

Take responsibility for enhancing your own employability:

1   Keep a track of any ways in which recruitment methods for your sector change.
2   Who are the key players in the market you're in for recruitment? Who are the main agencies?

3   Don't stay with an employer if they're not enabling you to meet your career goals. Do what you can to ensure that the doors to your advancement are truly shut – and then leave. You could be surprised.

Chapter 10

Here's to life!

Take a holistic view of your life, and good health and happiness are more likely to be yours. Take a narrow, focused view of it, concentrating on only one aspect, and the others areas will suffer. There will be times when one aspect of your life – such as your career – takes priority over others. But that doesn't mean that the rest of your life should lose out totally. If you're not fit and healthy for example, it will be harder to maintain a peak performance at work – which could make all the difference to whether you get that promotion or make that next step or not. Continually look at your life to consider questions such as:

- What do you want in your life besides your career?
- Who do you want in your life?
- What are you doing to enjoy life?
- What are you doing to pay off your loans?
- What are you doing to start building financial security for yourself?

We just have one life, so make time for those things which matter to you most, such as family, friends and fun. The way you manage your resources – time, energy, money, health and relationships – can make a huge difference to the quality of life you enjoy.

What are the things you want in your life to be happy and fulfilled? Do any of the examples in Table 10.1 below feature?

From the day we are born, life often gets in the way, throwing trials, tribulations and challenges at us. Working towards some 'wants' and 'must haves' in your life may demand that you 'park' other things aside for several weeks or months while you focus on them or a project that is of particular importance to you – such as your wed-

Table 10.1

Family – perhaps children	Key relationships and roles
Pets	Fun and laughter
Friends	Volunteering
Travel	Cultural and leisure activities
Dreams	Nature
Adventure	Excitement
Material goods	A good sex life
Achievements	Nice place to live
Financial assets	Solid retirement plans
Health and vitality	Great memories
Spirituality	Other

ding day or training for a marathon. But a balance helps keep things in perspective. And the work–life balance becomes a hot topic as individuals struggle to find ways to cope with the demands of work and personal commitments to family and friends. Balance is important in many aspects of life and Table 10.2 below gives suggestions as to where this balance is important.

How balanced is your life?

Every year, check your work–life balance is as you want. Assess how content you are with each area of your life which is important to you and to pinpoint those which need work and which you want to change.

Try this exercise to assess how well balanced your life is. For each of the categories you ticked above consider the questions:

1 How satisfied are you right now with each one? Rate them individually from 0 to 10. Totally satisfied earns a 10; complete dissatisfaction a 0.

Table 10.2

Work	and	Leisure
Work	and	Holidays
Rest	and	Exercise
Healthy food	and	A bit of what you fancy
Smooth running of life	and	Challenges
Certainty	and	Uncertainty

2   How does your life look? How many segments are a 10?
3   Which ones need working on (i.e. are below a 7)? What would
     they have to be like for you to rank them as a 10?
4   What do you need to do to make that happen?
5   What will you do to make them happen and when?

You can keep doing this exercise over and over, enabling you to make the changes you want in your life through a continual process of making sure that every one is a 10, or at least working towards it. In addition, you can repeat the exercise breaking down one element into various segments or units and grading each of them out of 10. Health and fitness might be divided into areas such as fitness, healthy eating, chill time, stretching and flexibility and smoking.

But work's taken over my life!

More employees are now finding that short breaks recharge their batteries quite adequately without a huge panic about sorting out the in-tray before and after a longer break. A good proportion put off their holidays and don't take the full allowance, *'I'm too busy at work'*. Very few of us can keep going at premium performance without having some sort of regular break built into the day. Our own bodies have their own needs; one person may be able to do with very little sleep, while others need a lot. If you don't listen to your body, sooner or later it will pay you back when you least need it, to remind you that it has needs too, such as *proper* rest and recuperation. You're not indispensable. It's sad to say, but if you were killed by a bus today, your company *would* go on without you. If you don't look after yourself, you are unlikely to be able to take care of others.

There are some careers in which long hours are the norm, but it can be easy to fall into the trap of doing long hours for the sake of it. The person who never takes a lunch break can rarely work at the same performance level throughout the day. The person who always takes a break away from the phone, email and work environment can only find her performance enhanced. No excuses! Walk around the block for 20 minutes and boost your heart beat, reduce your stress levels, keep that weight down *and* boost your mood.

Stress

With all the hype about stress, remember that the right sort of stress can help you live longer. Mild to moderate stress increases the production of brain cells, enabling them to function at peak capacity, so if you want to live life to a peak performance, get stressed but in the right way – it makes your body and mind stronger.

Beneficial stress gives you recovery time and a sense of accomplishment afterwards. It challenges you, although you may complain about it at the time. The bad stuff is prolonged, repeated, sustained and unrewarding. You need to find the gap somewhere between the two and build it into your daily life. Look for activities which reward and stimulate you, such as a run before work, studying in the evenings or voluntary work at weekends.

Get out of your comfort zone and take part in something which isn't routine and predictable or effortless. The more you look for these sorts of activities, the more you'll benefit. Collapsing in front of the TV after a day's work with a glass of wine isn't beneficial. Playing some sort of sport or going to adult education is. It's important to face stress or challenges mentally, physically, socially and spiritually. Give yourself proper 'chill' time. Don't waste time dwelling on the problems and demands of life – think about the pleasure, variety and vigour that challenges bring us and you'll feel much more alert and in control. Many challenges arrive through the roles we choose to play in life.

What roles do you want to play?

We all have roles in life and they all tend to appear at different times. Table 10.3 below shows roles most of us experience in our lives.

Our roles and relationships and the responsibilities that come with them intertwine with careers more than any other aspect of life. Which comes first: career or ageing relative? The presentation or a sick child? The school play or your squash game? The carer in us may play a key role and take centre stage in our lives while our parents get older and need decisions to be made for them. The parent has a lifelong role, but spends more time on it in the early years of a child's life and that role changes as life progresses, such that their children become their friends in adulthood. Our relationships with our siblings change, too, particularly as we all settle down into adult life and face the challenges of dealing with ageing parents.

Table 10.3

Parent	Friend
Son/daughter	Volunteer
Manager	Leader
Supervisor	Confidante
Doer	Thinker
Teacher	Adviser
Loner	Niece/nephew
Aunt/uncle	Grandparent
Actor	Diplomat
Neighbour	Carer
Sister/brother	Cousin
Good Samaritan	Hero

Our friends, too, change. We keep some throughout life; others we see enter at different stages and then leave, as if they came for a reason. Perhaps they were there to teach us something, to make us laugh at a time when we felt low, to make us feel good about ourselves, or just ... because. We need friends, both on our own account and when with a partner. Friends help you to keep things in perspective. A true friend is there for the good and bad times and will see you through.

If we're to have successful, empowering relationships, we need to put boundaries on what we will and won't do in our role. We may tire of the friend who calls us just once too often in the early hours of the morning, distraught over a break-up. We may be fed up of being the only sibling who makes an effort with our parents, while our siblings bleat that they are 'too busy'. Assertiveness is important if friendships and relationships are to thrive and grow. Saying 'no' is important in any role, if we are to feel strong and right. Saying 'yes' to keep the peace usually leads to feelings of resentment and disappointment in ourselves for not having the courage to say what we really want to say. Saying 'no' is a sign that we feel confident enough in ourselves to say what we mean and, crucially, that we care about ourselves and what we undertake in life.

The ability to manage yourself and others impacts on your ability to be personally effective in work and life. For example, if you have children, you will need to motivate them and get the family working as a team on projects to create a cohesive family unit. There will be times when you need to manage your own temper, when they do something which drives you to distraction for the hundredth time. Similarly, you will need to manage your client relationships at the office. If someone asks you for a piece of work which you know you cannot do within the timescale they give you, you will need to manage that and talk to them about it. You've learnt to manage people, situations and life at university and in your past life experience.

Develop your ability to handle people

1　Identify your boundaries in any relationship – the rules you feel comfortable with and stick to them.
2　Look at things from the other person's point of view. Put yourself in their shoes to get an idea for how they are feeling.
3　Remember that you cannot change other people – but you certainly *can* change the way you behave towards them.
4　Work on what you know you *can* influence, as opposed to the things you cannot.

Use your resources effectively

We have a tremendous amount of resources at our disposal, from mind-mapping to help creativity, speed reading to enable us to acquire knowledge more quickly, our memory to help retain it, meditation to help us focus and exercise to boost our energy. But the thing most people want more of today is time.

Is your time management letting you down?

'I haven't got time', is a common complaint. And yet how often do you reassess the way in which you spend your time (and money)?

- Track the ways in which you spend your time;
- Look back at your wheel of life and the activities you identified as important to you;
- How much of the 168 hours a week do you spend on them?
- Decide what to do about any imbalance;
- Track the way you spend your time for a week. In particular, track the time you're wasting on any of the activities in Table 10.4 below.

Table 10.4

Negative people/thoughts	Missing deadlines
Unanswered messages	Difficulty communicating
Outstanding letters and bills	Computer illiterate
Lacking confidence	Non-assertiveness
Unnecessary texting/emailing	Information overload
Losing things, e.g. keys	Smoking
Surfing the Internet	Drink and drugs
Broken items	Gambling
Too much TV	Fears
Poor sleep	Anxieties
Flitting from one thing to another	Doubts
without any real focus	Unnecessary meetings

Identify the three which waste most time for you and how much time they take up. What difference would it make if you didn't spend time on them? What are you doing to do to get rid of them and what will you do with your time instead?

Undertake exercises like this while you're still at university, when you've graduated and later on when you have work, family and house maintenance responsibilities, when you are commuting and studying for professional qualifications, and have social and leisure activities to fit in. You can also apply it to your working day to find out how you can use your time more effectively at work.

Do the same exercise with money

- ◆ What financial base do you want to build up in the future?
- ◆ What do you need to do to make that happen?
- ◆ What is getting in the way?

Identify the financial resources you want and then you can start making them happen. Some items are essentials, such as a property to rent or buy, living costs and tax and state demands, e.g. national insurance. After that, saving is usually a wise move for that rainy day, and so is insurance. There are also a whole range of investments, savings accounts, stocks and shares which are best discussed with a financial adviser.

Ten ways to review your finances continually

1   Where is your money going?
2   Which items are essential, important, nice to have?
3   Where can you cut back?
4   What will you do to make that happen?
5   Which items do you no longer need and could sell?
6   How could you make more money? Examples include focusing on career development so that your salary increases.
7   Who can help you sort out your debts and finances?
8   What do banks and building societies offer graduates?
9   What realistically can you achieve in the next week, six months and three to five years? How can you capitalise on that? Put any unexpected windfalls such as a bonus or present into paying off your loan straight away.
10 How rigorously are you making your money work for you?

Make your money work for you. Be proactive in looking for the best deal, the highest interest rates which suit your needs, the lowest loan rates, and keep looking. Do a three-monthly financial MOT and reward yourself for your financial acumen. The higher you climb the career ladder, the greater the perks and salary. Working for professional qualifications at night will not only boost your employability but also keep you away from expensive bars and nightclubs, keep your money in your pocket and enable you to pay off your loans and debts faster.

Most people continually believe they are short of time and money, but don't proactively do enough specifically about it. It takes discipline, effort and creative thinking to sort out your finances. Paying off a loan doesn't take forever, even though it may seem like it. Much depends on *how* focused you are in paying off your loans. And if you nurture your career, your financial status should get better as you're rewarded for your efforts. Careers take up around 48 weeks a year out of 52 and subsequently impact on your overall quality of life, so surely they are worth the effort and dedication?

Living at home with your parents after university?

Many young people are moving back home after university to save money, to pay off debts and for an assortment of other reasons.

But what other options do you have apart from moving back in with your parent(s)? Could you get in touch with other graduates in the area or on the same graduate trainee scheme in your company who are in the same boat and flat-share, or live abroad in a country where graduates are welcomed and it is easier to get on the housing ladder? If you still decide to return home (perhaps you never left), work out a financial arrangement so that you pay your parent(s) rent (even if it is a very small amount) – you need to keep in the habit of budgeting for your housing. And arrange with them what your contribution will be towards the house-keeping, be it cleaning, washing, helping in the garden, cooking a meal a couple of times a week. Don't fall back into the ways of a teenager having everything done for you. You've moved on from that and so have your parents, so don't use your parents' home: sit up, take some responsibility and *contribute* to it. Sit down and agree a few house rules (just as you would have had at university with your flat mates) to keep everyone happy and remember to practice the art of negotiation and compromise. Finally, consider these questions:

- How long do you intend to stay with your parents? Give yourself a deadline to leave and stick to it. Do you want to be living with them when you're 40?
- How much of your student debt will you have paid off by that time? How will you do it?
- What will you have achieved in your career by then and how will that have boosted your income to help you start building a financial base?

Finally, when the time does come to move out, why not get your parents a small gift as a token of appreciation for their help over the years? Parents are usually very happy to help out their offspring – but it is always nice to be appreciated and thanked.

Don't forget the wild and wacky

What would your life be like if you drew up a list of all the things you wanted to do and achieved before your eightieth birthday? What a glorious blaze of memories you could have to look back on as your older years set in!

List the things you want to do and the reasons *not* to do them will fade into the background. You'll be filled with a tremendous energy and enthusiasm, passion and excitement as you start identifying how and when you're going to do it all. Writing your list down enhances your determination to make your items happen. Keep your list where you can easily see it *frequently*. Show your list to those who are important to you in your life. Suggest they draw up a list of their own, and compare notes. Are there things you can do together? Can you give each other the time and space required to make them happen? You need to make sure that those you love don't constrain you in a plant pot, so that your roots can't spread out and grow. If they do limit you, it may be time to say farewell to the relationship. A rich relationship should enable you to take some journeys as a couple and others alone.

Don't become a robot

It's easy to fall into a continuous cycle of work, supper, TV, bed. The more you do, the more you'll want to do and the dream list above can help you do just that! And as you push back your boundaries outside work, it will also become much easier to do just that in your working life. At the start of this book, you identified what success and happiness meant to you. Perhaps you listed things like a large bank account, exotic holidays, happy, healthy kids who stay off drugs and alcohol; giving something back to the community which really makes a difference, a particular status in the community or organisation.

You need to decide how important success is to you and in what capacity. Occasionally, you may tweak or transform your ideas of success and happiness or completely change them. But in the hustle, bustle and noise of life, take time out to dream and look into the present and future to ensure you're spending your life on activities which, and with people who, are important to you. Get focused and create the life and success you want.

Looking forward

The goal posts of life are for your own positioning. Be clear about the things you want to change in your life and what you want out of it, and then take personal responsibility to make it happen. You may need to work around barriers and obstacles, and take regulations and rules into account along the way, but the journey makes the end achievement all the more rewarding.

Your degree over, you have a chance to look back, contemplate, reflect and congratulate yourself, and to look forward, to plan and build your future. Pause to do this at regular intervals in your life and it will feature the activities and achievements which are important to you.

Finally, consider what really is important in life. Do any of these elements feature for you?

1   Love and be loved;
2   Be passionate about a cause;
3   Wonder at the beauty of the earth and nature's sheer power;
4   Feel at peace;
5   Laugh and see the funny side;
6   Care for those you know and those you don't;
7   Be curious: don't lose the habit of asking what, why, when, where, who, how;
8   Learn from those who've gone before you and who'll come after you;
9   Use your creativity and imagination to the full;
10   Create you own luck, success and happiness.

And remember:

Nobody ever said: 'I wish I'd spent more time at the office' on their deathbed.

Summary action points

Your life
Your future
Your choice
Good luck!

Further reading

Careers related

AGCAS special interest series, available from your university careers service:
- *Using Languages*, AGCAS Information Booklet
- *Working Abroad*, AGCAS Information Booklet, Biennial
- *Working in Europe*, First Steps, AGCAS Information Booklet, Biennial.

Alexander, L. (2003) *Turn Redundancy to Opportunity*, Oxford: How To Books Ltd.

Angell, R. (2004) *Getting into Films and Television*, Oxford: How To Books Ltd.

Barrett, J. and Williams, G. (2003) *Test Your Own Aptitude*, London: Kogan Page Ltd.

Britten, A. (2004) *Working in the Music Industry*, Oxford: How To Books Ltd.

Brown, C. (2005) *Working in the Voluntary Sector*, Oxford: How To Books Ltd.

Brown, S. (2003) *Moving on Up*, London: Ebury Press

Kent, S. (2005) *Careers and Jobs in the Media*, London: Kogan Page Ltd.

Lees, J. (2005) *How to Get a Job You'll Love*, London: McGraw-Hill.

Williams, N. (2004), *The Work We Were Born to Do*, London: Element Books Ltd.

The Writers and Artists Yearbook, London: A&C Black.

The Writers' Handbook, London: Macmillan.

Further study

Marshall, S. and Green, N. (2004) *Your PhD Companion*, Oxford: How To Books Ltd. Contains a great selection of tips and advice to help you through your PhD.

Recruitment

See the website www.alec.co.uk for lots of formats and examples of CVs.

Bishop-Firth, R. (2004) *CVs for High Flyers*, Oxford: How To Books Ltd.

Bryon, M. (2005) *Graduate Psychometric Test Workbook*, London: Kogan Page Ltd.

Johnstone, J. (2005) *Pass that Interview: Your Systematic Guide to Coming Out On Top*, Oxford: How To Books Ltd.

Yate, M.J. (2002) *The Ultimate CV Book*, London: Kogan Page Ltd.

Yate, M.J. (2003) *The Ultimate Job Search Letters Page*, London: Kogan Page Ltd.

Yate, M.J. (2005) *Great Answers to Tough Interview Questions*, London: Kogan Page Ltd.

Moving up the career ladder

Bishop-Firth, R. (2004) *The Ultimate CV for Managers and Professionals*, Oxford: How To Books Ltd.

Hughes, V. (2004) *Becoming a Director*, Oxford: How To Books Ltd.

Purkiss, J. and Edlmair, B (2005) *How To Be Headhunted*, Oxford: How To Books Ltd.

Shavick, A. (2005) *Management Level Psychometric and Assessment Tests*, Oxford: How To Books Ltd.

Working abroad

Carte, P. and Fox, C. (2004) *Bridging the Culture Gap: A Practical Guide to International Business Communication*, London: Kogan Page Ltd.

Doing Business With, an excellent series published by Kogan Page Ltd covering these countries: Bahrain, Croatia, Saudi Arabia, UAE, China, Jordon, Kazakhstan, Kuwait, Lybia, Serbia and Montenegro and the EU Accession States.

Going to Live in ...and *Living and Working in* ...two highly informative and practical series published by How To Books Ltd (Oxford), covering countries such as Spain, Australia, New Zealand, France, Italy and Greece.

Khan-Panni, P. and Swallow, D. (2003) *Communicating Across Cultures*, Oxford: How To Books Ltd.

Reuvid, J. (2006) *Working Abroad: The Complete Guide to Overseas Employment*, London: Kogan Page Ltd.

Vacation Work have a plethora of publications which give you ideas on how you can go and work your way around the world. Visit www.vacationwork.co.uk.

Self-employment

Blackwell, E. (2004) *How to Prepare a Business Plan*, London: Kogan Page Ltd.
Bridge, R. (2004) *How I Made It: 40 Entrepreneurs Reveal All*, London: Kogan Page Ltd.
Gray, D. (2004) *Start and Run a Profitable Consultancy Business*, London: Kogan Page Ltd.
Isaacs, B. (2004) *Work For Yourself and Reap the Rewards*, Oxford: How To Books Ltd.
Jolly, A. (2005) *Fromm Idea to Profit*, London: Kogan Page Ltd.
Power, P. (2005) *The Kitchen Table Entrepreneur*, Oxford: How To Books Ltd. Turn that hobby into a profitable business!
Reuvid, J. (2006) *Start Up and Run Your Own Business*, London: Kogan Page Ltd.
Whiteley, J. (2003) *Going for Self-Employment*, Oxford: How To Books Ltd.

Gap year/time out

Potter, R. (2004) *Worldwide Volunteering*, Oxford: How To Books Ltd.
Vandome, N. (2005) *Planning Your Gap Year*, Oxford: How To Books Ltd.

Career and life success

Drummond, N. (2005) *The Spirit of Success*, London: Hodder and Stoughton.
Ebury, S. (2003) *Moving On Up*, London: Ebury Press.
Hill, N. (1996) *Think and Grow Rich*, New York: Ballantine Books.
Robbins, A. (1991) *Awaken the Giant Within*, New York: Simon and Schuster.
Tracy, B. (2003) *Goals! How to Get Everything You Want – Faster Than You Ever Thought Possible*, San Francisco: Berrett-Koehler Publishers Inc.

Learning skills

Bradbury, A. (2006) *Successful Presentation Skills*, London: Kogan Page Ltd.
Claston, G. and Lucas, B. (2004) *Be Creative*, London: BBC Books Ltd.
Covey, S. (2005) *The 7 Habits of Highly Effective People: Powerful Lessons in Personal Change*, London: Simon & Schuster UK Ltd.
Lilley, R. (2006) *Dealing with Difficult People*, London, Kogan Page Ltd.
Parsloe, E. (1999) *The Manager as Coach and Mentor*, London, CIPD.
Quillam, S. (2003) *What Makes People Tick?* London: Element.

Wiseman, Dr R. (2004) *The Luck Factor: Change Your Luck – and Change Your Life*, Sydney: Random House Australia (Pty) Ltd.

Managing others

Charney, C. (2001) *Your Instant Adviser: The A–Z of Getting Ahead in the Workplace*, London: Kogan Page Ltd.
Morris, M.J. (2005) *The First-Time Manager*, London: Kogan Page Ltd.
Taylor, D. (2005) *The Naked Leader*, London: Bantam Books.
Whitmore, J. (2002) *Coaching for Performance*, London: Nicholas Brealey Publishing.

Building financial bases

Ahuja, A. (2004) *The First-Time Buyer's Guide*, Oxford: How To Books Ltd.
Bowley, G. (2005) *Making Your Own Will*, Oxford: How To Books Ltd.
Chesworth, N. (2004) *The Complete Guide to Buying and Renting Your First Home*, London: Kogan Page Ltd.
Palmer, T. (2005) *Getting Out of Debt and Staying Out*, Oxford: How To Books Ltd.

Life related

Fortgang, L.B. (2002) *Take Yourself to the Top*, London: Thorsons.
Gaskell, C. (2000) *Transform Your Life – 10 Steps to Real Results*, London: Thorsons.

Useful addresses and further information

UK general

Association of Graduate Careers Advisory Services
Administration Office
Millennium House
30 Junction Road
Sheffield S11 8XB
Tel: 0114 251 5750
www.agcas.org.uk

Hobsons
www.hobsons.com
A website with lots of features to help you get that right job wherever you are

Prospects
www.prospects.ac.uk
A huge source of information and useful links for graduates of every discipline

UK regional graduate websites

Many of the sites below are designed to help graduates returning to the region or wishing to move to the area:
Yorkshire and Humber Region: www.graduatelink.com
Graduates Yorkshire: www.graduatesyorkshire.info
Graduates North East: www.graduates.northeast.ac.uk
Merseyside-Business Bridge www.business-bridge.org.uk
Merseyside: www.gieu.co.uk
Merseyside Workplace: www.merseyworkplace.com/
North West Student and Graduate On-Line: www.nwsago.co.uk

North Midlands and Cheshire Employers Directory: www.soc.
staffs.ac.uk/eh1/emp2003.html
Staffordshire Graduate Link: www.staffsgradlink.co.uk
Graduate Advantage – West Midlands: www.graduateadvantage.
co.uk
Gradsouthwest.com: www.gradsouthwest.com
GradsEast: www.gradseast.org.uk
The Careers Group, University of London: www.careers.lon.ac.uk
Graduate Ireland: www.gradireland.com
Scotland Graduate Careers, managed by Services to Graduates
Group: www.graduatecareers-scotland.org
Scotland – Graduates for Growth: www.graduatesforgrowth.co.uk
GO Wales: www.gowales.co.uk

Work experience, internships and voluntary work

Act for Tibet
www.actfortibet.org
Information and ideas of ways that you can support His Holiness
the Dalai Lama in his non-violent campaign for the people of Tibet

BUNAC
Dept PR1
16 Bowling Green Lane
London EC1R 0QH
Tel: 0207 251 3472
www.bunac.org.uk
A wide range of working holidays

Council on International Educational Exchange
www.ciee.org.uk
Long-term career-related placements or summer jobs in the USA,
teaching placements in Asia, adventure working holidays in
Australasia

Do It!
www.do-it.org
Find out what opportunities there are to volunteer in the region
you live in

GO Wales
www.gowales.co.uk

Graduate Business Partnership
Run by the University of Exeter
www.ex.ac.uk/businessprojects

Knowledge Transfer Partnership
www.ktponline.org.uk/graduates

Merseyside-Business Bridge
www.business-bridge.org.uk

www.gieu.co.uk
Merseyside-related programme of events to enhance your employability and prepare you for a competitive job market with representatives from various sectors

National Council for Work Experience
Tel: 0845 601 5510
www.work-experience.org
enquiries@work-experience.org

West Midlands Graduate Advantage
www.graduateadvantage.co.uk

Voluntary Service Overseas
Carlton House
85 Upper Richmond Road
London SW15 2BS
Tel: 0208 780 7600
www.vso.org.uk

Further study

Association of MBAs
25 Hosier Lane
London EC1A 9LQ
Tel: 0207 246 2686
www.mbaworld.com
Has a full list of accredited MBA courses, plus links to institutions,
and details of the MBA fair, scholarships, awards loans. The Official MBA Handbook can be acquired over their site and gives you

all the information you need to get started. There's also information about rankings

BLIS courses
www.blis.org.uk/courses
Courses and language finder supported by Learndirect and maintained by CILT

British Council
10 Spring Gardens
London SW1A 2BN
Tel: 0207 930 8466
www.britcoun.org
The British Council has a network of offices throughout the UK and in 110 countries worldwide. Visit its website or one of its offices for more information on funding, scholarships and studying in the UK. You will also find a lot of information about arts, science and society in the UK

www.direct.gov.uk/cdl
Information on Career Development Loans applicable to vocational courses only

National Union of Students
www.nusonline.org.uk

Ploteus
www.europa.eu.int/ploteus
The European course search portal

UKNARIC
Oriel House
Oriel Road
Cheltenham
Gloucestershire GL50 1XP
Tel: 0870 990 4088
www.naric.org.uk
The National Recognition Centre for the UK and National Agency for the Department for Education and Skills. The only official information provider on the comparability of international qualifications from over 180 countries

Post-graduate study and research

Arts and Humanities Research Council (AHRC)
Whitefriars
Lewins Mead
Bristol BS1 2AE
Tel: 0117 987 6543
www.ahrc.ac.uk

British Academy
www.britac.ac.uk

Association of University Language Centres in Britain and Ireland
www.aulc.org/aims.html

Find a Phd
www.findaphd.com
This website is the largest directory of PhD opportunities in the UK

Higher Education and Research Opportunities in the United Kingdom
www.hero.ac.uk
An excellent section on research with links to the main research councils, universities and others. Plus information on how to disclose your findings as a new researcher

Languages Research
www.languagesresearch.ac.uk
An online source of reference for research interests in modern language studies across the UK

National Post-Graduate Committee
www.npc.org.uk
The NCP represents the interests of post-graduate students in the UK. Information on funding, discussion boards, post-graduate facts and issues, and post-graduate careers. Also an academic job search with international links to jobs in the USA, Canada and Australia among others

Research Councils
www.research-councils.ac.uk
A partnership set up to promote science, engineering and technology supported by the eight UK Research Councils. Grants are

allocated to individual researchers, networks of people working on projects, programmes, designated research centres, fellowships and post-graduate students.

The Royal Society
www.royalsoc.ac.uk

The United Kingdom Research Office (UKRO)
www.ukro.ac.uk
The leading information and advice service on EU research and higher education

Universities UK
www.universitiesuk.ac.uk

Self-employment

British Franchise Association
Thames View
Newton Road
Henley-on-Thames
Oxon RH9 1HG
Tel: 01491 578 050
www.thebfa.org
For information on franchises, both in and outside the UK, finding a franchise, successful case studies and events, a list of members. Ask for a copy of the British Franchise Association Franchisee Information Pack and check when the next Franchise Exhibition is near you on its website

BusinessLink
www.businesslink.gov.uk
A network of business advice centres in England with allied bodies in Scotland, Wales and Northern Ireland, all accessible through this site

Prime Initiative
Astral House
1268 London Road
London SW16 4ER
Tel: 0208 765 7833
www.primeinitiative.org.uk
Dedicated to helping those over 50 to set up their own business

Prince's Trust
Tel: 0800 842 842
www.princes-trust.org.uk
Help for the 14–30 year old who wants to set up his or her own business or tackle barriers to employment

Shell LiveWIRE
www.shell-livewire.org
Unlock your potential with this excellent site. Plus financial action planning and a fabulous business encyclopaedia. For 16–30 year olds who want to start and develop their own business

Start-ups
www.startups.co.uk

Protecting your creativity

ACID – Anti Copying in Design
www.acid.uk.com

Institute of Trade Mark Attorneys
www.itma.org.uk

Own It
www.own-it.org

Patent Office
www.patent.gov.uk
For details on how to apply for registration, design, copyright and trade marks

Usability Professionals' Association
www.upassoc.org

Job sites

The Artists Information Company
www.a-n.co.uk
Jobs and opportunities for subscribers plus advice about making a living from the arts

www.artsjobsonline.com
Advertising arts jobs in the UK and Ireland, a relatively new site and blissfully simple to use, for job seekers or employers

Get a Life
www.getalife.org
Careers guidance and information for the public sector

The Guardian
http://media.guardian.co.uk/
Provides the latest news and links to recruitment sites with a huge jobs section

Ideasfactory.com
www.ideasfactory.com/careers
Lots of invaluable information and links about the creative industries

The Knowledge
www.theknowledgeonline.com
Database of useful contacts in film, TV and video production

www.mad.co.uk
This online magazine of the art and design trade publications encompasses Marketing Week, Instore Marketing and Design Week

Jobs in the media industry
National Campaign for the Arts
www.artscampaign.org.uk
Represents all the arts.

Spotlight
www.spotlightcd.com
Publishes casting directories in constant use by film, TV and theatrical companies

The Stage
www.thestage.co.uk
For people who want to get into the industry but also pulls together those already working in it with vacancies, mostly of a technical nature but also general arts

Training bodies

The Council for Advancement of Communication with Deaf People
(British Sign Language Interpreting)
Durham University
Science Park, Block 4
Stockton Road
Durham DH1 3UZ
Tel: 0191 383 1155
www.cacdp.org.uk

Centre for Information on Language Teaching and Research (CILT)
20 Bedfordbury
London WC2N 4LB
Tel: 0207 379 5101
www.cilt.org.uk
See also:
www.languageswork.org.uk
Languages work with lots of information about careers and work
with languages

Languages National Training Organisation
20 Bedfordbury
London WC2N 4LB
Tel: 0207 379 5101
www.languagesnto.org.uk
The NTO merged with CILT (see above) to promote greater
national capability in languages in the UK

National Council for Drama Training
1–7 Woburn Walk
London WC1H 0JJ
Tel: 0207 387 3650
www.ncdt.co.uk
info@ncdt.co.uk

Periodicals Training Council
Periodical Publishers Association
28 Kingsway
London WC2B 3DA
Tel: 0207 404 4166
www.ppa.co.uk

Publishing Training Centre
Book House
45 East Hill
London SW18 2QZ
Tel: 0208 874 2718
www.train4publishing.co.uk

Regional Language Networks (UK)
www.cilt.org.uk/rln
Supporting CILT's mission to boost language capability in the UK

Royal National Institute for the Deaf (RNID)
19–23 Featherstone Street
London EC1Y 8SL
Tel: 0207 296 8000
www.rnid.org.uk

Skills for Media (New Media Careers Information service from Skillset and BECTU)
Skillset, The Sector Skills Council or the Audio Visual Industries
Prospect House
80–110 New Oxford Street
London WC1A 1HB
Tel: 0207 520 5757
Skillset Careers Information Service on 08080 300 900 (England) and 0808 100 8094 (Scotland)
www.skillset.org.uk
www.skillset.org/freelance for freelancers to train

For information about working in the media

National Film and Television School
Beaconsfield Studios
Station Road
Beaconsfield
Bucks HP9 1LG
Tel: 01494 671 234
www.nftsfilm-tv.ac.uk

FT2 (Film and Television Freelance Training)
3rd Floor
18–20 Southwark Street
London SE1 1TJ
Tel: 0207 407 0344
www.ft2.org.uk

Job sites

International

www.asia.hobsons.com
Careers in Asia from Hobsons with regional outlooks

www.blis.org.uk/jobs
BLIS Jobs, a site for people with languages, maintained by CILT, the National Centre for Languages

www.eurolondon.com
The consultancy for all language recruitment

www.europa.eu.int/eures
EURES, the European job mobility portal

www.french-selection.co.uk
Jobs for French, German and Spanish speakers

www.gaijinpot.com
Jobs in Japan, mostly English teaching and some IT jobs

www.jac-recruitment.co.uk
Jobs for Japanese speakers

www.latpro.com
Jobs in the Americas requiring English, Spanish and Portuguese

www.lingojobs.com
Jobs for bilingual and multilingual job seekers in the UK and other European countries

www.linguistsdirect.com
www.mcable.net
For language, translating and other writing jobs

www.multilingualvacancies.com
An online network for people seeking bilingual jobs

www.monster.co.uk
Lists many jobs using languages in the UK and other European countries and more

www.people-first.co.uk
Recruiting supply chain, multilingual and Japanese speakers

www.prospects.ac.uk
Country specific information

www.reed.co.uk
Lots of graduate vacancies online with plenty of good advice

www.talent4europe.com
A site featuring jobs in all EU countries

www.toplanguagejobs.co.uk
In London, UK and Ireland

www.workinjapan.com
For those of you who would like to work in Japan

www.workpermit.com
Lots of information about immigration and visas worldwide

UK

www.ft.com
Financial Times newspaper

www.timesonline.co.uk
The Times

www.getalife.org.uk
Careers guidance and information for the public sector

www.joslinrowe.co.uk
Joslin Rowe, with lots of opportunities in the financial services sector, including accountancy, finance and office support. It has global alliances in Australia, New Zealand, South Africa, Poland and more. It has a Working Worldwide Guide

www.officeteamuk.com
OfficeTeam have offices in the UK, Australia, Canada, New Zealand, plus the USA and various European countries. They place

staff in administrative roles including HR, customer services, PA and office manager

www.irecruit.co.uk

www.languagebuisness.co.uk
Customer services, IT helpdesk, financial support, administration and secretarial, market research and telemarketing, account management, sales and marketing and data editing, predominantly in London and the Home Counties, but with some opportunities overseas for those of you with language skills

www.naturalbornbillers.co.uk
Sales, marketing and customer service for bilingual speakers

Universities, colleges and school

www.jobs.ac.uk
The official recruitment website for staffing in higher education

www.jobs.tes.co.uk
The *Times Educational Supplement* with lots of vacancies in education

ETeach
www.eteach.com

www.linguistlist.org
Academic jobs involving languages and linguistics

International organisations

European Language Council
http://web.fu-berlin.de/elc
Aims for the improvement of knowledge of language and cultures in the EU and beyond
Freie Universität Berlin
ZE Sprachlabor
Habelschwerdter Allee 45
14195 Berlin
Germany
Tel: +49 30838 53718

UNESCO
7 Place de Fontenoy
75352 Paris
France
www.unesco.org

Professional organisations and trade associations

The following are examples of professional and trade associations which relate to business and finance. Many have international links with their peers abroad, so research their websites thoroughly

International organisations

Creative Clusters
www.creativeclusters.com
An international conference and network for people working in the development of the creative industries

Culture Base
www.culturebase.net/mission.php
A database an international source on international artists, performers and promoters

Visiting Arts
Bloomsbury House
74–77 Great Russell Street
London WC1B 3DA
Tel: 0207 291 1600
www.visitingarts.org.uk
For visiting artists to the UK

UK based

Creative and Cultural Skills
11 Southwark Street
London SE1 1RQ
Tel: 0207 089 5866
www.ccskills.org.uk

Acting

British Actors Equity Association
Guild House
Upper St Martin's Lane
London WC2H 9EG
Tel: 0207 379 6000
www.equity.org.uk

Independent Theatre Council
12 The Leathermarket
Weston Street
London SE1 3ER
Tel: 0207 403 1727
www.itc-arts.org
admin@itc-arts.org
Represents performing arts organisations

Advertising

Advertising Association
7th Floor
Artillery house
11–19 Artillery Row
London SW1P 1RT
Tel: 0207 340 1100
www.adassoc.org.uk
aa@adassoc.org.uk
You can download the AA's careers guide *Getting Into Advertising* from its website

Advertising Producers Alliance
47 Beak Street
London W1F 9SE
Tel: 0207 434 2651
www.a-p-a.net
info@a-p-a.net

CAM Foundation Ltd
(Communications and Marketing Education Foundation)
Moor Hall
Cookham
Maidenhead
Berks SL6 9QH
Tel: 01628 427 120
www.camfoundation.com
info@camfoundation.com

European Association of Communication Agencies
EACA Secretariat
152 Blvd. Brand Whitlock
B-1200 Bruxelles
Tel: (32-2) 740 07 10
www.eaca.be

Institute of Practitioners in Advertising
44 Belgrave Square
London SW1X 8QS
Tel: 0207 235 7020
www.ipa.co.uk

Arts

Arts Advice
Tel: 0800 093 0444
www.artsadvice.com

Arts Council England
14 Great Peter Street
London SW1P 3NQ
Tel: 0845 300 6200
www.artscouncil.org.uk

Arts Council of Wales
Museum Place
Cardiff CF10 3NX
Tel: 029 2037 6500
www.artswales.org.uk

Arts Marketing Association
7a Clifton Court
Clifton Road
Cambridge CB1 7BN
Tel: 01223 578078
www.a-m-a.co.uk
info@a-m-a.co.uk

Northern Ireland Arts Council
77 Malone Road
Belfast BT9 6AQ
Tel: 028 9038 5200
www.artscouncil-ni.org

Scottish Arts Council
12 Manor Place
Edinburgh EH3 7DD
Tel: 0131 226 6051
www.sac.org.uk

Booksellers

Booksellers Association of United Kingdom and Ireland
Minster House
272 Vauxhall Bridge Road
London SW1V 1BA
Tel: 0207 802 0802
www.booksellers.org.uk

Design for business

UK Web Design Association
Fareham Enterprise Centre
Hackett Way
Fareham
Hampshire PO14 1TH
www.ukwda.org

These sites may also be useful:
www.britishdesign.co.uk: British Design Innovation
www.bedg.org: British European Design Group

www.cfsd.org.uk: Centre for Sustainable Design
www.dba.org.uk: Design Business Association
www.designinbusiness.org.uk: Design in Business
wwwdesignmuseum.org: Design Museum
www.dffn.org: Design for Future Needs
www.designinparliament.org.uk: Parliamentary Design Group
www.webdesignforbusiness.org: Design for Business

Government

Local Government Careers
www.lgcareers.com: for more careers information
www.lgjobs.com: for current job vacancies in councils

Foreign and Commonwealth Office
Recruitment Section
Human Resources Directorate
Room 2/89
Foreign and Commonwealth Office
Old Admiralty Building
Whitehall
London SW1A 2AH
www.fco.gov.uk
Plus information on embassies abroad and in the UK, travel alerts, scholarships and fellowships, and links. The site also has very useful country profiles

Higher education

Association of University Teachers
Egmont House
25–31 Tavistock Place
London WC1H 9UT
Tel: 0207 670 9700
www.aut.org.uk

Subject Centre for Languages, Linguistics and Area Studies
www.ilas.ac.uk
Promotes high quality learning and language teaching across all UK higher education institutions

www.ucml.org.uk
University Council for Modern Languages, the membership organisation for higher education language lecturers and associations

Illustrators

Association of Illustrators
2nd Floor
Back Building
150 Curtain Road
London EC2A 3AR
www.theAOI.com

The Society of Illustrators (USA)
www.societyillustrators.org

Journalism/Writing

Hold the Front Page
Invaluable links for journalism at www.holdthefrontpage.co.uk

Association of Author's Agents
www.agentsassoc.co.uk

Society of Editors
University Centre
Granta Place
Mill Lane
Cambridge CB2 1RU
Tel: 01223 304080
www.societyofeditors.co.uk

British Association of Journalists
89 Fleet Street
London EC4Y 1DM
Tel: 0207 353 3003
www.bajunion.org.uk

Newspaper Society
74–77 Great Russell Street
London WC1B 3DA
Tel: 0207 636 7014
www.newspapersoc.org.uk

National Union of Journalists
Headland House
308–312 Gray's Inn Road
London WC1X 8DP
Tel: 0207 278 7916
www.nuj.org.uk

Scriptnaked
Lighthouse
9–12 Middle Street
Brighton BN1 1AL
Tel: 01273 384 222
www.scriptnaked.org.uk/
Offers professional development opportunities for aspiring and
practising screenwriters

Society of Authors
84 Drayton Gardens
London SW10 9SB
Tel: 0207 373 6642
www.societyofauthors.net

The Editorial Centre
Tel: 01424 435 991
www.editorial-centre.co.uk
As part of the Press Association Group, the Editorial Centre runs
courses in journalism for beginners and experienced journalists,
also in photography, sub-editing and video journalism, sports
writing and feature writing

Writers Guild of Great Britain
15 Britannia Street
London WC1X 9JN
Tel: 0207 833 0777
www.writersguild.org.uk

Language and literature specific

Assocation Internationale des Interprètes des Conference (AIIC)
International Association of Conference Interpreters
10 Avenue de Sécheron
CH-1202 Geneva
Switzerland
Tel: +41 22 908 15 40
www.aiic.net
Nearly 3,000 members in 250 cities throughout the world

Association of Translation Companies (ATC)
5th floor
Greener House
66–68 Haymarket
London SW1Y 4RF
Tel: 0207 930 2200
www.atc.org.uk

British Association for Applied Linguistics
www.baal.org

Canadian Association of Second Language Teachers
www.caslt.org
Lots of useful worldwide links

CALICO
Computer Assisted Language Instruction Consortium
Texas State Univesrity
214 Centennial Hall
St Marcos
Texas 78666
USA
Tel: +1 512 245 1417
http://calico.org

Chartered Institute of Linguists
Saxon House
48 Southwark Street
London SE1 1UN
Tel: 0207 940 3100
www.iol.org.uk
info@iol.org.uk

The Institute of Linguists, which serves the interests of professional linguists worldwide
European Confederation of Language Centres for Higher Education
www.cercles.org

The Institute of Translation and Interpreting
Fortuna House
South Fifth Street
Milton Keynes MK9 2EU
Tel: 01908 325250
www.iti.org.uk
The independent professional association of practising translators and interpreters in the UK

International Federation of Translators
2021 Union Avenue
Suite 1108
Montreal
Quebec H3A 2S9
Canada
Tel: +1 514 845 0413
www.fit-ift.org

National Register of Public Service Interpreters
NRPSI Ltd
Saxon House
48 Southwark Street
London SE1 1UN
Tel: 0207 940 3166
www.nrpsi.co.uk
nrpsi@iol.org.uk

Metropolitan Police Test
Language Services Ltd
Tel: 0207 397 8770
www.languagesservicesltd.com
info@languageservicesltd.com

Translators Association
84 Drayton Gardens
London SW10 9SB
Tel: 0207 373 6642

Multimedia

British Interactive Multimedia Association
Briarlea house
Southend Roead
Billericay CM11 2PR
www.bima.co.uk
info@bima.co.k

Photography

Association of Photographers
81 Leonard Street
London EC2A 4QS
Tel: 0207 739 6669
www.the-aop.org
general@aophoto.co.uk

British Institute of Professional Photography
Fox Talbot House
2 Amwell End
Ware
Herts SG12 9HN
Tel: 01920 464 011
www.bipp.com

Printing

Institute of Paper, Printing and Publishing
83 Guildford Street
Chertsey
Surrey KT16 9AS
Tel: 0870 330 8625
www.ip3.org.uk

Scottish Print Employers Federation
48 Palmerston Place
Edinburgh EH12 5DE
Tel: 0131 220 4353
www.spef.org.uk

Public relations

Chartered Institute of Public Relations (CIPR)
PR Centre
32 St James's Square
London SW1Y 4JR
Tel: 0207 766 3333
www.ipr.org.uk

Public Relations Consultants Association
Willow House
Willow Place
London SW1P 1JH
Tel: 0207 233 6026
www.prca.org.uk

Publishing

Association of Learned and Professional Society Publishers
South House
The Street
Clapham
Worthing
West Sussex BN13 3UU
Tel: 01903 871 686
www.alpsp.org

DPA
Queen's House
28 Kingsway
London WC2B 6JR
Tel: 0207 405 0836
www.directory-publisher.co.uk

Publishers Association
29B Montague Street
London WC1B 5BW
Tel: 0207 691 9191
www.publishers.org.uk

Society for Freelance Editors and Proofreaders
Riverbank House
1 Putney Bridge Approach
Fulham
London SW6 3JD
Tel: 0207 736 3278
www.sfep.org.uk

Recruitment and employment

Recruitment and Employment Confederation
36–38 Mortimer Street
London W1W 7RG
Tel: 002 7462 3260
www.rec.uk.com

Teaching

Association of Language Learning
150 Railway Terrace
Rugby CV21 3HN
Tel: 01788 546 443
www.all-languages.org.uk

Association of Recognised English Language Services (ARELS)
56 Buckingham Gate
London SW1E 6AG
Tel: 0207 802 9200
www.englishuk.com
Information on events and training, jobs and resources

Eurydice
www.eurydice.org/
The information network on education in Europe

Training and Development Agency for Schools
Portland House
Bressenden Place
London SW1E 5TT
Tel: 0845 6000 991
www.tda.gov.uk

Visit www.fasttrackteaching.gov.uk if you want to be a leader in education in England at primary, secondary or special schools

Teaching English as a Second Language in Australia
www.ueca.com.au

Television and film

BBC Recruitment Services
PO Box 48305
London W12 6YE
www.bbc.co.uk/jobs

BECTU (Broadcasting Entertainment, Cinematograph and Theatre Union)
373–377 Clapham Road
London SW9 9BT
Tel: 0207 346 0900
www.bectu.org.uk
info@bectu.org.uk

British Kinematograph Sound and Television Society
The Moving Image Society
Pinewood Studios
Iver Heath
Bucks SL0 0NH
Tel: 01753 656 656
www.bksts.com
info@bksts.com

CFP Europe
Bernhard Bangs Allé 25
2000 Frederiksberg
Denmark
Tel: +45 33 86 28 91
Fax: +45 33 86 28 88
www.cfp-e.com
cfp-e@cfp-e.com

Channel 4
Human Resources Department
124 Horseferry Road
London SW1P 2TX
www.channel4.com

five
22 Long Acre
London WC2E 9LY
www.five.tv

British Film Institute
www.bfi.org.uk

ITV Network Ltd
200 Gray's Inn Road
London EC1X 8HF
www.itv.com/jobs

Lighthouse Arts and Training Ltd
9–12 Middle Street
Brighton BN1 1AL
Tel: 01273 384 222
www.lighthouse.org.uk
Offers professional development opportunities for screenwriters,
artists, and filmmakers working with digital and moving image
media

The Script Factory
Welbeck House
66–67 Wells Street
London W1T 3PY
Tel: 0207 323 1414
www.scriptfactory.co.uk
Supports the screenwriting industry by finding and developing new
talent, amongst other things

Skillset
Prospect House
80–110 New Oxford Street
London WC1A 1HB
Tel: 0207 520 5757
www.skillset.org.uk
The sector skills council for the audiovisual industries

Theatre

Association of British Theatre Technicians
55 Farringdon Road
London EC1M 3JB
Tel: 0207 242 9200
www.abtt.org.uk

Society of British Theatre Designers
55 Farringdon Road
London EC1M 3JB
Tel: 0207 242 9200
www.theatredesign.org.uk